Nature and Therapy

Recent decades have seen an increasing interest in the healing and therapeutic potential of nature and the potential of green care interventions for the benefit of mental health. The field of nature-based therapies is expanding in line with this interest. *Nature and Therapy: Understanding counselling and psychotherapy in outdoor spaces* offers a unique contribution by outlining the specific processes involved in conducting counselling and psychotherapy sessions in outdoor natural environments.

Central areas covered in the book include:

- a thorough exploration of the evidence for the psychological and healing potential of natural spaces;
- developing a therapeutic rationale for nature-based therapeutic work;
- understanding the therapeutic relationship and the unique therapeutic processes that come into play in outdoor natural spaces;
- translating indoor therapeutic work to outdoor contexts;
- the practicalities of setting up and running a therapy session outside of a room environment;
- experiential exercises to explore the therapeutic potential of nature.

Martin Jordan offers a clear outline of how to set up and hold a therapeutic session outdoors. Using case examples, *Nature and Therapy* explores both the practicalities and the therapeutic processes that come into play in an outdoor natural setting. The book will be of use to counsellors, psychotherapists, arts therapists, psychologists and health professionals who are interested in taking their therapeutic work into natural environments and outdoor spaces.

Martin Jordan is a chartered counselling psychologist, UKCP registered psychotherapist and counsellor. He is also a senior lecturer in counselling and psychotherapy and course leader for the postgraduate diploma in psychodynamic counselling at the University of Brighton, UK.

Nature and Therapy

Understanding counselling and
psychotherapy in outdoor spaces

Martin Jordan

Routledge
Taylor & Francis Group

LONDON AND NEW YORK

First published 2015
by Routledge
27 Church Road, Hove, East Sussex, BN3 2FA

and by Routledge
711 Third Avenue, New York, NY 10017

Routledge is an imprint of the Taylor & Francis Group, an informa business

British Library Cataloguing in Publication Data
A catalogue record for this book is available from the British Library

Library of Congress Cataloging-in-Publication Data
Jordan, Martin, 1967–
  Nature and therapy : understanding counselling and psychotherapy in
  outdoor spaces / Martin Jordan. – Dual First.
      pages cm
  1. Counseling. 2. Psychotherapy. I. Title.
  BF636.6.J67 2014
  158.3–dc23   2014013680

ISBN: 978-0-415-85460-3 (hbk)
ISBN: 978-0-415-85461-0 (pbk)
ISBN: 978-1-315-75245-7 (ebk)

Typeset in Times
by Keystroke, Station Road, Codsall, Wolverhampton

To Cara, Gemma and Mary with all my love

Contents

Figures

Foreword

It is fitting that this fascinating piece of research has been based in Brighton – which (in 2014) has the only Green council and only Green Member of Parliament in the UK. Brighton has the reputation for being a home for creative and innovative people, hosting an annual festival of arts and sponsoring a thriving culture, where artists and designers open their houses and studios to the public for three weekends during the festival. We are also fortunate to retain within the city large open spaces, gardens, parks and allotments. There are exciting projects to develop derelict areas into community gardens, although in the face of fiercely contested competition from supermarkets and other commercial developments. A whole area of Brighton, the run-down London Road, is being redeveloped to include new student accommodation behind a preserved Art Deco façade, an enlarged and redesigned Open Market, a historic space called The Level which now houses a skate park, café and rose garden yet retains plenty of lawn where people can relax, walk their dogs and children can play in safety. Not least, the amazingly eccentric Royal Pavilion with its gardens, lawns and outdoor café – the last being the subject of an enormous petition to preserve it. I realise how privileged we are if we live in an environment where we can enjoy both green spaces and a lively city, with easy access to both sea and the Sussex Downs. I use the term 'privileged' because this is unfortunately not an experience that a lot of people enjoy. They do not have a lot of choice about where they live and work. It may be rather 'gritty' and overcrowded, with few areas of green. However, that is not to say their space isn't as much loved and appreciated as the lawns and gardens of other places. As a city child myself, transported at the age of six into a remote woodland setting on the edge of a village, the shock was immense. However, the advantages of exploration, making camps, studying the wildlife, disappearing for hours on end to collect frogs for my pond (yes even at that age!) quickly became evident. Nevertheless, I was afraid of the trees at night, having read *Jack the Giant Killer* and imagining the trees coming alive. The woods then became dangerous, 'nature' was transformed into something menacing. If the sky turned cloudy, I would rush home before I could get caught by the suddenly threatening arms of the trees. I do not think our family ever got over the feeling of being 'exiled' even though there had been a choice about moving.

In the early days of discussing Martin's project, we constantly returned to the question of 'nature' and 'natural' as being understood as something beneficial. Indeed, there are precedents in the history of education for romanticising the countryside, for establishing schools for children with emotional difficulties in the Cotswolds, for example, with the assumption that being removed from an inner-city environment into these 'idyllic' places would have a positive impact on their behaviour and well-being. Sometimes it did, probably because of the novelty, and the dedication of the staff, but sometimes it was a disaster. So what is a therapeutic space for one can be hellish for another. My aunt and mother, evacuated from the East End as young women during the Second World War, were so traumatised by the Somerset village and its inhabitants that they quickly returned to London. Famously, my aunt was heard to say: 'I would rather put up with Hitler and his bombs than stay with that bunch of snobs . . .' She also retained a fear of cows and horses that lasted all her life.

So what has this to do with the theme of Martin's book, taking therapy outside, into nature? I think a lot, for with any shifts in a way of thinking should come questioning of assumptions, with serious reflection concerning why, how, pros and cons.

In the world of psychotherapy, in particular psychoanalysis, the convention has been to conduct sessions in a space with clear boundaries, such as the consulting room. This space is often within a purpose-built centre and may be a shared office with desk, chairs, computer, filing cabinets, or a fairly impersonal carpeted room. Or it could be in the therapist's home, where most people would have some evidence of their lifestyle visible. Pictures, carpets, furniture, ornaments – these are owned by the therapist and may be of considerable interest to the client but are often not discussed. Freud's consulting room must have been a wonderful treasure house for his clients, but probably not so unusual in Vienna at that time. He had a couch, covered with an oriental carpet, and lots of valuable artworks and orna-ments. He did not sit face to face with the client, and to imagine him going out into a Viennese park with his client would be hard. Over time, many psychoanalysts have, either for convenience (no room for a couch) or preference, changed to conducting therapy face to face, sitting on chairs. They will usually adhere to the fifty-minute hour though. The client is in effect a visitor and usually respects the space. At the end of the session, the client will get up and leave the room. Failure to do so would be interpreted in any number of ways. After a short interval, another client will come in. I would say this was a usual pattern for most private practices. In sunny weather, both parties might think that they would prefer to be outside. In high wind and rain, this is unlikely. Much of the literature emphasises the concept of 'safe space' – a knowable, predictable place where both parties understand their roles and the boundaries. When clients are feeling emotionally vulnerable, some stability is important. It is also the same for the therapist who can rely on that known space.

But Martin wanted to start conducting psychotherapy outdoors! As someone for whom being outside in the 'natural' world, the landscape of mountains, rivers, changing skies, plants and animals, is extremely important, he wanted to understand what would happen if he followed his inclination and began to do therapeutic work 'outside'. There were some indications that therapists involved with ecopsychology and global environmental protection had begun to consider this as a possibility as well. Why not then consider bringing a passion for being in nature into work as a psychotherapist? So began the long road to exploration, reading the literature on outdoor therapy, adventure therapy, wilderness therapy, talking to colleagues who had made a similar decision, continuing to reflect on his own practice, taking into account the clients' views, talking to other therapists, such as art therapists, for some of whom the decision to work outside was not so radical; being challenged at every turn concerning the assumptions in some of the literature that 'going outside' or being in remote spaces would be beneficial; above all, considering how the 'frame' would be significantly changed if the boundaries of the consulting room were not there. What would that do to the relationship between client and therapist if both were outside in all weathers, having to negotiate a different kind of boundary? Would that make the whole process of therapy more 'democratic'?

Rather than simply 'getting on with it', which could have been an easier option, Martin undertook a serious and systematic piece of research, on which this book is based. I asked him, do you see this 'therapy outdoors' as a new modality or as one development that could happen in any of the many psychotherapy modalities? Is special training required? What would the impact be on current training programmes if 'therapy outdoors' becomes more accepted? These are questions that need to be continuously explored as given the often claustrophobic spaces that therapists are required to work in, within the public sector, 'going outside' might be both practical and desirable. I remember the first time I accidentally 'went outside' whilst running an art therapy workshop in Switzerland. The training programme had recently been relocated from its inner-city premises to an area surrounded by woodland. The trainees were emphatic that they wanted to work outside, given that the weather was warm and sunny. I thought, why not, mainly because I was frankly reluctant to be inside as well and because the trainees had clearly done this before and seemed confident. We had to negotiate the boundaries of the workshop space (within calling distance of the building and therefore of each other), work in small groups, with people to remain with their groups, and all this with the concept of safe space in our heads. In that relatively confined area this did not seem a problem and indeed the environments that were created using the resources of the woodland were stunning. But, in some of Martin's examples, therapy is taking place in remote regions, involving some precarious management of terrain, inclement weather, potential for injury of one party or the other. How would we square health and safety requirements of our professional bodies with such practice?

In this book, the reader will find a combination of solid practical illustration in the context of a wide range of literature and philosophical reflection. Martin's contribution to the professions of psychotherapy and counselling, and including the arts therapies, is a very timely and courageous one with the potential to lead to further research and a significant shift in theory and practice.

Professor Diane Waller OBE
Emeritus Professor of Art Psychotherapy, Goldsmiths, University of London
Principal Research Fellow, School of Applied Social Science,
University of Brighton
Art Psychotherapist and Group Analytic Psychotherapist

Preface

This is a 'how to' book. My aim in writing the book is to support other therapists who are interested in taking their therapeutic work outdoors into natural settings, by giving some guidance on issues which need to be considered when working in a unique and different setting from the room. My main aims are fourfold; first, 'how to' understand the role of nature in the therapeutic process and relationship by a thorough exploration of what 'nature' might be and the role it might play. Second, 'how to' understand the pragmatics of setting up and conducting therapeutic work outdoors, with a specific emphasis on the holding of the therapeutic frame in this new setting, something I feel hasn't been adequately done in the literature to date. Third, 'how to' understand aspects of the therapeutic process that seem to come into play in the outdoor natural setting and how to work with these. Lastly I wanted to support therapists in understanding 'how to' develop their own therapeutic relationship to nature in order to translate this experience into their work. A different therapist trained in a different modality from me would quite possibly have placed greater or lesser emphasis on some things, and anyone reading the book will, I am sure, be doing this dependent on their own unique preferences and bias in the ways in which they work. In this way the book is a 'how to' map, a cartography which will be interpreted and understood from a number of different perspectives. Please take from it what is useful to you and respectfully coexist with what may not be so useful to you. I hope you find the book enjoyable.

Acknowledgements

As with any acknowledgements it is difficult to know where to start. To Cara for all the support in giving me time to write and her generosity of spirit. To Hayley Marshall for all the (continuing) conversations where we try to work out what is going on and why we are doing this. These conversations have been stimulating and enlivening and without them the book could not have been written. To all the therapists who were generous in giving their time in talking about their experiences in taking therapy outdoors; some of these stories appear in this book and form the backdrop to a lot of the understanding of taking therapy outdoors. To the members of CAPO – counsellors and psychotherapists outdoors for the times spent around a fire and in the yurt discussing the work, laughing, eating and drinking. To the clients I have worked with who have shared in the journey of moving outdoors and for sticking with it through rain and shine, warm and cold days alike. To my generous colleagues at the University of Brighton and in particular the counselling team for covering for me when I was lucky enough to take a sabbatical in order to write this book. A special thank you to the School of Lost Borders for a significant and formative experience in my journey outdoors into nature. To Chris, Richard and the men's group for the early days of support in facilitating my growing understanding of the healing power of nature. To Brenda Crowther, Jungian analyst, for showing me how to hold someone in a therapeutic relationship without unnecessary rigidity of thought and behaviour, and for all the work in helping me to understand my dreams. To Anna Maria and Eva in Sweden and all at Alnarp University for being so welcoming and interested in my research. To my mother and father, without whom I wouldn't have trained as a therapist, and to my ancestors who all had a role to play in getting me here.

Author's note

In relation to any outdoor work and before carrying out any of the ideas suggested in this book, readers should make sure health and safety regulations have been met and risk assessment requirements for outdoor activities have been carried out and you have adequate insurance to cover your therapeutic work. Neither the author nor the publishers take any responsibility for any consequences of action taken as a result of the following information which is contained in the book.

The case examples given in this book arise from work with individual clients where consent has been obtained to use details of therapeutic work carried out. Any identifying details have been removed to ensure anonymity of those involved.

Therapists' stories are taken from research undertaken by the author and where consent was given to publish accounts of the interviews. Names have been changed to protect the anonymity of those involved.

Introduction

In recent decades interest has grown in the relationship between our contact with the natural world and its effect on our emotional well-being. In discussions with family, friends and colleagues it would be hard not to find somebody who could talk about their relationship with the natural world, and the healing and beneficial effects it had upon them. It might be through activities in nature such as walking, cycling, camping or climbing, or they might talk about their enjoyment of gardening and growing plants and vegetables. They might speak about the impact of particular places they had visited locally, or on travels further afield, places that continue to have or have had a profound and healing effect on them. They might even use the language of spirituality or existentialism, saying that these experiences create a deeper sense of connection with the more-than-human world. They might express how their connection to nature allowed them to see their place in the universe as part of a greater interconnected whole. Whatever the experience, there is a large body of people for whom contact with nature is very important. In talking to people about their relationship to nature, there might also be anxieties around what is happening to the natural world: resource depletion, global warming, unfolding natural catastrophes, and the impact of overpopulation and environmental degradation. Their emotional reaction to this may cause a sense of depression and hopelessness, a fear that we are sleepwalking into a catastrophe.

There may also be people who you know or see in your clinical practice as a therapist, who suffer from seasonal affective disorders. As summer starts to fade, the nights draw in, trees shed their leaves, and the temperature drops, some people experience the shift towards winter and the shortening of days with a mild sense of unease. For others, this seasonal process may cause bigger shifts in their mood and well-being and result in more dramatic changes in their mental health, possibly requiring clinical support. It is clear that our relationship with nature (or lack of it) has an effect on our emotional and psychological well-being. Climate change now presents us with some very real environmental and psychological threats to our well-being. Some therapists have taken the problems that climate change presents us with as the central focus of their therapeutic and campaigning work. Seeing psychological and social transformation as interlinked, they position the role of counselling and psychotherapy as central in supporting people to make the shifts towards a more sustainable society and dealing with the emotional and psychological fallout from unsustainable ways of living.

This book aims to explore how this relationship to nature which gives rise to both positive and potentially negative feeling can be developed in the context of counselling and psychotherapy. At the time of writing this book, a new introduction to counselling has been published (McLeod 2013) which has a whole chapter dedicated to therapy in nature and using the outdoor environment for therapy. This is a major milestone and represents just how far the field has come and is developing. This book aims to make a contribution to the field, expanding understanding of how the practice and process of counselling and psychotherapy work in an outdoor natural setting.

My personal journey

Due to my personal experience of the healing effects of nature and my training as a therapist, I wanted to start to conduct psychotherapy outdoors, to take my clients into natural spaces such as parks, fields, woods and more mountainous terrain. I found that very little had been written about this specific activity: counselling and psychotherapy in outdoor natural contexts. Although there was a field of practice called adventure therapy and wilderness therapy, which sat alongside the emerging fields of ecotherapy and ecopsychology, there was no specific activity which could clearly be seen as counselling and psychotherapy in nature. As I went out into nature to practise psychotherapy, I struggled to understand how my training and practice indoors could transfer outdoors. I encountered a range of problems both practical and philosophical, raising big questions about what underpinning knowledge and understanding I could draw upon to inform my psychotherapy practice in the outdoors.

When I initially started to think about moving outside of the therapy room, I encountered a range of practical issues, including the weather, terrain and the physical safety of both myself and my clients. Alongside this I also encountered frame-based tensions of confidentiality, timing and conducting the process of therapy outside the confines of two chairs in a room. Concurrently with this I was wrestling with theoretical issues around how to understand the role the outside environment, particularly the natural world, played in the therapeutic process. I struggled to understand how the developmental and relational nature of psychological distress, as presented to me in narrative form and understood through processes such as transference and countertransference within the confines of the therapy room, translated to a natural outdoor space.

My own relationship to the outdoors and the natural world has developed over a number of years. From a young age I would go out into nature in the fields around my home in Essex to feel at peace and to escape tensions at home with my parents. I spent a lot of time alone on my bike cycling round the country lanes, going out to marshland and visiting the estuaries and rivers near where I lived. I also spent time with friends lighting fires and climbing trees. This all seemed natural as a child; the natural world was integral to much of my childhood play. As a teenager I spent less time in nature, but enjoyed being outdoors working on building sites and engaging in the physicality of work, digging holes and lifting and carrying building materials. At university I became interested in indigenous forms of healing and was lucky to study a course on shamanism taught by Brian Bates at the University of Sussex (Bates 1984) which fuelled my interest in Native American cosmology and healing practices. When I worked in a day centre with adults with learning disabilities I was involved in a project growing vegetables and working on the land where we had an allotment. As I trained as a therapist I concurrently engaged in a men's group who met in woodland and did sweat lodges and other practices of connection to nature. Due to this experience and my interest in Native American ideas I trained as a 'vision fast' facilitator at the School of Lost Borders (www.schooloflostborders.org). I have written about this experience (Jordan 2005), which had a powerful psychological effect on me, not wholly positive. All of these experiences grew into a personal process of enquiry whereby I sought to attempt to bring these interests to bear on my therapy training and practice. In 2007 I started to take both individual clients and groups outdoors into natural spaces in order to begin to try to work therapeutically with them.

In terms of moving outdoors there was a distinction between the three types of therapy that I practised. One was a traditional one-to-one set-up conducted on a weekly basis at a regular time and at the same place. The other work I engaged in was over a long weekend (from Friday to Sunday) with a group of up to ten participants, where we camped, ate and slept in the same vicinity. The context of these weekends varied from remote mountains in North Wales, to hill walking in the Peak District, to woodlands in the East Sussex countryside. I co-ran these workshops with another therapist. Finally I ran one-day workshops exploring the therapeutic potential of the natural world, which I called 'ecotherapy'. Both the weekends and day workshops predominantly used experiential exercises and group reflections to facilitate participants' connections and emotional experiences in relation to the natural spaces we were in.

When I moved outside in my one-to-one therapy, I experienced a range of challenges, initially focused around the practicalities. I worried about confidentiality, particularly in public outdoor spaces such as parks; this was less of an issue in more remote terrain such as hills and mountains, but still a possibility. To resolve this issue I found an outdoor space which mirrored the indoor space: a willow dome situated within a managed wild garden space (Figure 1); it was somewhere with an entrance where I could set up two chairs and have some control over who entered the space by putting up signs saying 'workshop in

Figure 1 The willow dome space where I practise one-to-one work (Photo: Author)

progress, do not disturb'. This enabled me to relax and be able to focus on the therapy without fear of interruption, although it was not failsafe, and occasionally I had to intervene when someone ignored the signs and entered the location. Through this process of trial and error I learnt to rethink the therapeutic contract, accounting for some of the issues in working in an outdoor terrain. These included what to do if it rains (sit under umbrellas or tarpaulin), or if it is too cold (regularly check with the client about levels of comfort), or if someone interrupts the work. I managed to account for this, both in written form via a contract for outdoor work, and I also verbally agreed with clients what to do in certain contingencies such as interruptions (I would get up and engage the person before they entered the willow dome and head them off).

When I initially went outdoors to conduct counselling I felt overwhelmed by the sensory overload of the moving space we encountered. The space we were in felt alive and vibrant, compared to the static space of the indoor room, which took some getting used to. Initially I found that I lost the clear threads of transference and counter transference that seemed more apparent within the indoor room space. In my one-to-one therapy work I dealt with this issue by sitting in the contained space of the willow dome. To some extent this mimicked the room space I was used to and meant that my ability to focus increased.

However at the same time I felt a growing incongruence with being in the outdoor space. If it was so like the indoor space, why go outdoors? If I wasn't foregrounding the natural world as an intrinsic part of the process, what was the point? Some of these issues have lessened as I have continued to work one to one in this outdoor space. One client has continued to stay with the process over subsequent years and as part of our work we have questioned and continued to discuss why go outdoors? What has always felt important for the counselling work I do is to verbally explore the client's inner object-relational world. When I questioned my client about how sitting in the context was working for her, she answered that she found the context of nature relaxing and healing. What has developed in this one-to-one work is that my client can choose where to sit in the wild garden space around the willow dome. These choices and movements have mirrored her inner emotions and have allowed us more freedom than in an indoor space. I also now regularly walk and talk with my clients, conducting sessions whilst walking in natural locations.

My own practice in this context has helped me understand the work on different levels. Rather than a therapeutic nature 'out there' to connect to, there has been a more subtle movement between inner and outer worlds that has enhanced the work and allowed me to think beyond the confines of focusing either entirely on inner subjective feelings or solely on the outside. Through this experience and my theoretical reading, I became interested in the space between subjectivity and objectivity and how it can be understood in outdoor therapy experiences. In the same way I became interested in the process of therapy as movement, and how this movement could be understood both as an interior and exterior process.

When I conducted group work over long weekends, I struggled in different ways. A series of challenges came to the fore as part of working therapeutically outdoors in a wider range of contexts. Certain environments presented physical risks such as rough terrain and steep ground with the potential for exposure to more hazardous weather. If I had been operating within an adventure therapy process then these issues would have become challenges that clients could overcome, mirroring internal difficulties that needed to be addressed. At times, for example camping in high winds, things became quite challenging. However the process of these weekends was much more focused on therapeutic relationships, and the difficult weather became a phenomenon that mirrored internal relational processes, provoking emotional responses within participants. The idea that 'you can't control the weather' mirrored the process that we cannot always control the emotional weather of our lives and relationships. Other natural phenomena provoked existential concerns about seeing ourselves as a small part in a wider evolving universe. However, for me, the most challenging aspect of these weekends was managing the therapeutic process of the group alongside the physical issues of camping in difficult terrain: I felt I had to wear two hats, sometimes at odds with one another. On one weekend we were using a chemical toilet as no toilet facilities existed, and at the end of the weekend I had to literally deal with the group's shit! I found these physical as well as emotional aspects of the weekend exhausting. By being with the group over a long weekend I also found my own role shifted and changed as well as the affective spaces the group inhabited. At times we were in a designated therapeutic space, sharing experiences in a circle, while at other times we were in social spaces eating and talking. I struggled with how to negotiate these spaces and what role I had at different times in relation to the group: therapist, guide, first aider, 'waste manager', cook, etc. Different geographical contexts also felt different: woods and mountains have the capacity to evoke different affective processes. The outdoor environment has the capacity to mobilise different affects in relation to internal worlds, for example woodland environments can feel more holding and containing.

The ecotherapy days allowed me to focus specifically on the therapeutic effects of contact with the natural world. Alongside presenting issues of confidentiality, weather, physical comfort, etc., I began to question 'what is nature?' as the space we were in (I used the willow dome for the majority of these workshops) was more of a hybrid version, with paths, managed woodland and parks, fences, allotments and horticultural projects, none of which evoked a 'pure' natural context. I started to research this area and developed through my reading the concept of an 'emerging post-nature' (Anderson 2009), which seemed to fit more with what I was experiencing. These reflective experiences, coupled with the theoretical readings and challenges I encountered, have all contributed to the interpretive lens I brought to writing this book.

As part of this process I sought out others who were trying to work therapeutically in nature. I joined peer groups of interested practitioners who were working in a range of contexts attempting to utilise the therapeutic potential of nature. Through these meetings I met another psychotherapist, Hayley Marshall, who like me was attempting to take her therapeutic practice outdoors. We have spent the last six years talking about this process and the therapeutic work with our clients, trying to figure out what was happening in the new contexts and how the therapeutic process and relationship shifted and changed in an outdoor setting. This culminated in an article we wrote (Jordan and Marshall 2010) which discussed how we saw the therapeutic frame and therapeutic process working in this new setting. This book is both my personal account of this work and also a continuation of my work with Hayley and others involved in understanding counselling and psychotherapy outdoors, including members of the Counselling and Psychotherapy Outdoors group (see www.outdoortherapy.org.uk).

Map of the book and chapters

Chapter 1 looks at the evidence and literature that support the idea of nature as a healing space. The three main theories from environmental psychology are covered here: the Biophilia Hypothesis, attention restoration theory and the psycho-evolutionary theory of stress reduction. The evolution of the green care movement is discussed and the growing position of counselling in nature as both aligned and unique in green care is outlined. Taking a broader definition of health and well-being, links are made between the growing theoretical movement of ecopsychology and how human health is intrinsically linked to planetary health. In doing this I discuss how important reconnective practices such as conducting therapy in nature are in understanding ecopsychology's project of reconnection to nature as central to mental health, and how disconnection may be at the root of some forms of mental distress. In the second part of this chapter I move into a fuller philosophical and theoretical discussion around the question of what is nature? I see this as funda-mental to understanding a position for nature that places it as central to why therapeutic work should be conducted outdoors, seeing human and nature located in a reciprocal process of relationality. Links are made between understanding nature as an unfolding, vital, dynamic process, both material and immanent, and how this might link to newer forms of understanding of the role of vitality in psychotherapy.

In Chapter 2, I explore the field of nature-based therapies. There are particular approaches to working therapeutically outdoors which provide a lot of useful insight; writings from the Natural Growth Project (Linden and Grut 2002), Nature Therapy (Berger 2006) and Nature Guided Therapy (Burns 1998) all provide theoretical and case discussion which can inform ways of working outdoors. There is also a growing and very informative body of literature emerging from the field of ecotherapy. However there are some specific areas in the literature that are not covered fully or in enough depth to support a therapist who, trained to work indoors, wants to understand the unique aspects of holding a therapeutic frame in an outdoor context and certain aspects of how the therapeutic relationship and process are affected by the move outside. The following chapters address this gap in understanding.

Chapter 3 looks at the therapeutic relationship from the perspective of relational psychotherapy. The relational approach offers a vehicle through which factors such as transference and counter transference and change processes can be understood in an outdoor context. Concepts such as 'implicit relational knowing' and 'moments of meeting' offer a way of understanding the therapeutic process and how it is affected within a dynamic moving environment. A case example is given to illustrate aspects of the unfolding therapeutic relationship within the outdoors; attachment patterns are explored and how they link to understanding of human–nature relationships. The chapter concludes by exploring the concept of nature as a transitional object and includes a case example to illustrate this.

In Chapter 4, I look at three central concepts in understanding therapeutic processes in nature. Participation in either active or passive forms helps us to understand how the experience of nature can be therapeutic on a number of levels and how participative processes can be utilised for therapeutic purposes. I then explore how projective processes, in particular the use of arts and metaphors, can be utilised to explore therapeutic material when conducting therapy outdoors. Finally I discuss the importance of both personal and transpersonal processes, how they link to seasonal and a deeper spiritual engagement with nature that can have a powerful therapeutic effect.

In Chapter 5, I look at some central practice issues in conducting counselling and psychotherapy outdoors in a safe, ethical and competent way. I look at the importance of the therapeutic boundaries in outdoor work and the importance of the psychological capability of the therapist in their ability to hold boundaries appropriately outside of the safety of the room context. In exploring the centrality of the frame, I outline how the frame shifts when moving into an outdoor natural setting. Assessing clients for their appropriateness for outdoor therapy is important and this is explored by giving a case example looking at factors important in clients' suitability for working in nature. I also outline the adaptions needed to the therapeutic contract and how to set up the pragmatics in an outdoor space, thinking about how to begin and end sessions. This is particularly important where the therapeutic space is more 'public' and potentially much less contained than it would be in a room setting. Confidentiality is then explored as a central issue and concern for outdoor therapy; this needs to be negotiated and discussed in contracting with clients for outdoor work and thinking about the impact of the weather on sessions. Finally I look at the importance of health and safety outdoors and some important factors to consider when assessing risks and maintaining both physical and psychological safety.

In Chapter 6, I review therapists' experiences in taking their therapeutic practice outdoors. This is done through reference to research interviews undertaken as part of a project exploring therapists' experiences of working outdoors. A central starting place and an important aspect of the therapeutic rationale for wanting to work outdoors, is the role of the natural world in the emotional and psychological life of the therapist. Several therapists had a strong and enduring history of going into natural spaces to restore themselves and to find emotional and spiritual solace. Some therapists were driven by a need to take on issues in relation to the current environmental crisis, seeing their therapeutic work as strongly linked to enabling people to develop a more ecological sense of themselves and their relationships. I look at how in taking their work outdoors therapists experienced anxieties, feeling they were breaking the rules of therapy and being transgressive; others worried about how to contain the work and how to keep it safe, both emotionally and physically. Some therapists struggled to understand the greater multidimensional nature of working outdoors and how to translate their predominantly indoor-based training into a new setting. Finally I look at how two therapists had experienced the shift and the unique perspectives they brought to understanding their work in this new setting. The stories are both unique in the therapists' passion and interest in moving outdoors, but at the same time they convey some of the joys and challenges faced by most therapists when they attempt to begin practising outdoors.

In Chapter 7, I look at ways in which a therapist can develop their own therapeutic relationship with nature. By exploring their historical relationship with nature and the emotional role it has played in their life, a therapist interested in working outdoors can begin to translate their own experience in order to develop a rationale for taking therapeutic work into nature. Several exercises are outlined to develop an engagement with nature through both the senses and the therapist's emotional life. Making reference back to Chapter 4 on therapeutic processes, I suggest ways in which the therapist can explore participative, projective and transpersonal therapeutic process through a range of experiential exercises.

References

Anderson, J. (2009) Transient convergence and relational sensibility: beyond the modern constitution of nature. *Emotion, Space and Society* 2, 120–127.

Bates, B. (1984) *The Way of Wyrd*. London: Book Club Associates.

Berger, R. (2006) Beyond words: nature-therapy in action. *Journal of Critical Psychology, Counseling and Psychotherapy* 6(4), 195–199.

Burns, G. (1998) *Nature Guided Therapy: Brief Integrative Strategies for Health and Well-Being*. London: Taylor & Francis.

Jordan, M. (2005) The vision quest: a transpersonal process. Paper presented to the British Psychological Society Transpersonal Psychology Section Conference, 17 September 2005.

Jordan, M. and Marshall, H. (2010) Taking therapy outside: deconstructing or reconstructing the therapeutic frame? *European Journal of Psychotherapy and Counselling* 12(4), 345–359.

Linden, S. and Grut, J. (2002) *The Healing Fields: Working with Psychotherapy and Nature to Rebuild Shattered Lives*. London: Francis Lincoln.

McLeod, J. (2013) *An Introduction to Counselling*, 5th edn. Milton Keynes: Open University Press.

Chapter 1

The healing effects of nature – why go outdoors?

One of the central issues in developing a therapeutic rationale for taking therapy outdoors is an understanding of the positive psychological effects of nature on human well-being. First I will look at three theories that locate nature's healing effects within a scientific evidence base and which have been referred to extensively in the literature. These theories attempt to capture, in empirical language and concepts, the 'feeling' of what nature does for us in terms of well-being and reduction in stress, and why we may be hard-wired in evolutionary terms to seek contact with the natural world. I will then review some supporting literature in terms of the green care movement and discuss the emerging field of ecopsychology. Ecopsychology positions relationships with nature within a reciprocal process which is intrinsically linked to mental health.

The Biophilia Hypothesis

A starting point for articulating the human–nature relationship has been the assertion of the Biophilia Hypothesis (Wilson 1984). The Biophilia Hypothesis is defined as the innate tendency to focus on life and life-like processes. Wilson believed that we were biologically programmed in terms of genetics to seek kinship with the more-than-human world. The Biophilia Hypothesis suggests human identity and personal fulfilment somehow depend on our relationship to nature. The human need for nature is linked not just to the material exploitation of the environment but also to the influence the natural world has on our emotional, cognitive, aesthetic, and even spiritual development. In further elaborating the Biophilia Hypothesis, Kellert (1993) points to the relationship between the historical development of the self, the natural environment and our genetic evolution as interdependent – that this evolutionary connection somehow resides in our genes. The Biophilia Hypothesis is often used to support the idea of an evolutionary relationship with nature that is not purely biological but is linked to psychology and identity.

Attention Restoration Theory (ART)

Focusing on the process of attention, Kaplan and Kaplan (1989) and Kaplan (1995) have researched the restorative effects of the natural environment, resulting in 'Attention Restoration Theory'. They undertook research which explored the psychological effects of being in both wilderness and nearby nature such as parks and woodland. Taking William James's concept of voluntary and involuntary attention, they explore how 'directed' attention which involves sustained concentration in a task whilst holding other distracting tasks at bay (for example whilst I am trying to write this at my computer I am wrestling with two distractions, whether I should make myself a coffee or whether I should walk the dog) affects us on a psychological level. They propose that these distractions have to be blocked out, and this causes tiredness and depletion in higher cognitive functioning. Being in natural environments involves a different sort of cognitive functioning, indirect attention or what is termed 'soft' fascination (Kaplan and Kaplan 1989). Soft fascination is maintained in an aesthetic and sensory contact with the natural world, by being away from the routines of our day-to-day life, and this needs to be compatible with our expectations of the trip and experience. This explains why not all trips into nature may be restorative, particularly if the weather turns bad or we get lost. For attention and restoration to occur, certain things need to be present in order for the restorative effects to be felt: being away from everyday work, access to complex ecosystems, trails and paths for exploration. The 'extent' of these environments in providing diversity and scope which engage us is important. This engagement then provides the psychological effect of fascination in relation to animals, birds, trees, plants and views. When the person partakes in compatible activities such as walking, bird watching and fishing, this all leads to a feeling of well-being and a felt restoration of attention and capacity. Overall the theory clearly outlines how contact with both wilderness and nearby natural environments allows us to feel restored and able to return to more complex urban environments.

Psychoevolutionary theory of stress reduction

In his classic paper on a view from a hospital window, Roger Ulrich (1984) compared the recovery of patients who had a view of a blank hospital wall with those who could see trees from their hospital beds. Data were analysed over a ten-year period on the duration of stay in hospital post-operatively for those recovering from gall bladder operations; perhaps unsurprisingly those who had a view of the trees had shorter stays in the hospital. Ulrich (1983) saw visual properties of natural environments, such as complexity and depth, as important, with a number of elements providing stimulation, such as an array of plants. A deflected vista – such as open savannah-like environments – is important, as is the presence of water. This environment needs to be appraised as one where threat is absent or negligible. All of these qualities are thought to rapidly evoke automatic positive affective and parasympathetic physiological responses with associated feelings of calmness, relaxedness, pleasantness and fascination (Ulrich 1983).

In summary, both Kaplan's and Ulrich's research has driven the development of restorative health environments such as the importance of placing gardens in hospitals and other places. There has been a growing body of research, particularly in Scandinavia, which has explored the design and implementation of rehabilitation gardens aiming to promote recovery from mental health problems such as stress and burnout (Stigsdotter and Grahn 2003).

What these different theories point to is the importance of nature in provoking an aesthetic and affective response which is positive and beneficial to human health in a number of ways: reducing stress, restoring attention, promoting well-being. It also highlights how contact with nature is driven by an unfolding evolutionary process linked to brain chemistry and genes which is essential for human survival.

Recent research on the effects of nature on brain chemistry has been emerging from Japan. This research, exploring the effect of Shinrin-Yoku (*taking the atmosphere of the forest*) on physiology, found that subjects experienced lower levels of the stress hormone cortisol after walks in the forest compared to walks in the laboratory (Tsunetsugu et al. 2007; Lee et al. 2011). This and other research coming from Chiba University, Centre for the Environment, in Japan, also found that subjects reported a sense of increased vigour and aliveness, and highlights nature's role in promoting a sense of psychological vitality (Selhub and Logan 2012).

There is a growing evidence base that points towards the role of nature and its preventative and curative effects. Frumkin (2012) has reviewed the current research in a number of areas in relation to clinical epidemiology – what determines health and disease in human populations. The research underlines the importance of contact with animals and the role of pets in human health and well-being, alongside the importance of plants, landscapes, and wilderness experiences. But Frumkin argues that we should treat this evidence with caution as there are still some questions that need to be answered more fully: for example, through what mechanisms does nature contact improve health and well-being? What forms of nature contact are most effective? What specific groups might benefit? He asks the question that is relevant for this book: does psychotherapy that employs nature (i.e. ecotherapy) have an empirical basis? His argument is that more empirical research needs to be undertaken to establish and support the role of nature in psychological health, and the effectiveness of approaches such as ecotherapy in utilising nature in the therapeutic process.

The green care movement

Taking counselling and psychotherapy outdoors can be located in a broad movement that has been growing over the past decades. This movement seeks to enlist the context and processes of the natural world in order to promote physical and psychological well-being, as well as recovery from physical and mental ill health. The 'green care movement' includes a number of interventions such as therapeutic horticulture, animal-assisted therapy, care farming, green exercise and wilderness therapy. Some of these activities have been brought together under the banner of 'ecotherapy', a term encompassing a broad range of therapy interventions aimed at intervening in mental health issues and promoting good mental health through contact with nature. A recent report 'Green Care: A Conceptual Framework' (Sempik et al. 2010) defines green care as a useful phrase summarising a wide range of both self-help and therapy programmes. The document aims to map out the different aspects of the potential for green care. The natural world is the framework within which green care takes place and is in this sense the common denominator amongst a wide variety of approaches and interventions. In the report Sempik et al. (2010) make a distinction between the active components of the majority of green care approaches like horticultural therapy and the 'passive' experiencing of nature which may not necessarily be green care. The report highlights the fact that there is plenty of research evidence to demonstrate correlations between well-being and green care settings but a lack of research to demonstrate actual cause and effect relationships between green care interventions and health and well-being.

This book situates itself within this broad movement seeking to further understand the therapeutic potential of nature, but at the same time locates counselling and psychotherapy as a unique therapeutic intervention within nature. Green care encompasses a broad range of 'care' interventions, and while these approaches are valuable in themselves to health and well-being, they do not necessarily foreground aspects of the therapeutic frame and therapeutic relationship in the same way that occurs in counselling and psychotherapy. My aim is to further understand the practice and therapeutic process of counselling and psychotherapy outdoors, exploring how important dimensions of the therapeutic frame, therapeutic process and therapeutic relationship shift when taking therapy outdoors. In this sense I aim to contribute to the area of green care referred to in the report as 'nature therapy', drawing from particular models of mind and forms of professional practice which are especially relevant to conducting therapy in nature. At the same time it is important to acknowledge the common factors highlighted in the green care movement, and not to position counselling and psychotherapy in nature (although unique) as an exclusive activity. It is clear that many common factors may also be present for both client and therapist working in nature, not least of which are the plants, animals and landscapes (Sempick et al. 2010). Alongside this there is the solace that nature gives both parties, contributing to enhanced positive effects in areas of well-being, psychological states, spirituality, a sense of peace and physical health. The 'Green Care' report also highlights the multifaceted nature of green care, that the benefits of the natural environment on health and well-being are mediated by a number of different mechanisms which do not sit in isolation from one another. Sempik et al. (2010) propose that these mechanisms may be operating simultaneously and/or sequentially, a multidimensionality which poses a challenge to research processes, especially if they are seeking to isolate contributing variables and factors.

Redefining health and well-being: dynamic, relational systems

One of the important strands of the concept of green care outlined in the report is the redefinition of health and well-being, which is not solely based on the absence of disease or illness. Introducing the relative model of health (Downie et al. 2000), which takes into account the importance of the multidimensional and subjective processes inherent in understanding individual well-being and ill health, Sempik et al. (2010) position health as a dynamic interactive and unfolding process. These processes are interconnected through physical, mental and social factors. According to the relative model of health, the perceived state of health is a dynamic process affected by individual subjectivity.

When this concept of a subjective, dynamic and unfolding process of health is placed in a relational framework within a natural environment, mental health can be located in a systemic interactional process, situating a relationship with the natural world as central to mental health. Gregory Bateson, one of the originators of systems thinking, has written about the importance of seeing mind as part of a relational and ecological system. In positioning the mind in relationship to nature, Bateson (1972) concludes that instead of Darwinian species taxonomies as both the unit and battlefield of survival, the unit of survival is organism plus environment. Thus thought becomes intrinsically linked to its environmental context, becoming what Bateson terms 'an ecology of mind'.

> There is an ecology of bad ideas just as there is an ecology of weeds, and it is characteristic of the system that the basic error propagates itself. It branches out like a rooted parasite through the tissues of life, and everything gets into a peculiar mess. When you narrow down your epistemology and you act on the premise 'what interests me is me, or my organisation, or my species', you chop off consideration of other loops of the loop structure. You decide that you want to get rid of the by products of human life and that Lake Erie will be a good place to put them. You forget that the eco-mental system called Lake Erie is part of your wider eco-mental system – and that if Lake Erie is driven insane, its insanity is incorporated into the larger system of your thoughts and experience.
>
> (Bateson 1972: 484)

Bateson presents us with a relational model of mind–nature communication, in that one does not make sense out of the context of relationship to the other. Next I will look at some of the theoretical perspectives that attempt to explore the importance of psychological connection and disconnection to the natural world, and the effects that this has on mental health.

Ecopsychology: the restorative power of mind–nature communication

One of the starting points in attempting to understand human–nature relationships in the form of ecological communication is the idea of *miscommunication* between humans and nature, leading to distress for humans, non-humans and ecological systems. The fields of scientific ecology and psychological understanding both need a meeting place, a space where ecological communication between mind and nature can emerge between disciplinary ideologies. The deep ecology movement originating from the ideas of Arne Naess (1973) proposed a move away from a shallow instrumental version of ecology, what Naess referred to as 'man in environment', towards the idea of a 'total field' of relationships. Deep ecology has had an impact on much ecopsychological theorising (Seed et al. 1993; Macy 2007). It is this meeting place which serves as the basis for placing humans back within the ecosystem and developing a sense of self in relation to this; what has been termed by some as an 'ecological self'.

One argument put forward by ecopsychology (Roszak et al. 1995) is that human psychopathology increases the more we find ourselves distanced from the environment. The more this ecological miscommunication persists, the more ecological systems seem to be in disarray, as evidenced by growing concerns about climate change and how this may affect (and is affecting) planetary ecological systems. Kidner (2007) has argued that the increasing rates of depression, a growing worldwide public health concern, are a direct result of a growing disconnection from the natural world. Beginning with industrialisation, our concepts of self and identity have shifted to fit a growing dislocation from land, agriculture, seasonal processes and fluxes; and the resultant individualisation and materialistic value system leaves us, Kidner argues, with an increasing sense of anxiety and depression.

Ecopsychology has attempted to position the psyche as both needing to connect with the environment and suffering from the results of this disconnection. Ecopsychology exists at the interface between several different disciplines which themselves have radically different epistemological and ontological foundations. Ecopsychology finds a home within psychology, environmental philosophy, ecology and environmental activism; although its relationship to psychology is a complex one, as it sits between a humanistic/transpersonal paradigm (Schroll 2007; Greenway 2010; Metzner 1995; Reser 1995) and a more experimental paradigm advocated by branches of conservation and environmental psychology (Reser 1995; Clayton and Myers 2009). However, psychology as a field is contested, with several competing ideas and paradigms. One of the central tenets of ecopsychology is the articulation and examination of the emotional and psychological relationship with the natural world, and the reciprocal effects of human and natural world interaction. The fundamental challenge that presents itself to ecopsychology is to locate the human 'mind' in some form of relationship with the natural world and to understand this relationship as reciprocal.

There is a long history of articulating the field of ecopsychology, from a number of writers (Boston 1996; Schroll 2007; Scull 2009; Greenway 2010). However I especially want to locate ecopsychology within complex systems of thought which are emerging at this time in history. Ecopsychology will benefit from being understood in relationship to the pre-modern, modern and postmodern systems of thought which have forged its birth. However finding a 'core' language to represent ecopsychology as a unified discipline is problematic, and it might best be seen as a location for thought, language and practical action that is attempting to articulate the human–nature relationship.

Roszak's initial vision for ecopsychology sought to place the psyche back into the context of the earth, 'the physical matrix that makes living intelligence possible' (Roszak 1992: 320). He outlines some of the principles of ecopsychology, arguing that life and mind emerge via evolution within an unfolding sequence of the physical, biological, mental and cultural systems; and proposing that the core of the mind is the ecological unconscious, a place where inherent reciprocity and connection to the natural world exist as the core of our being and through industrialisation have been repressed, resulting in madness and rampant ecological destruction. Roszak acknowledges that the idea is 'speculative', but no more so than the rest of the field of psychology (Roszak et al. 1995: 14). In linking ecopsychology to psychotherapy, Roszak states that:

> Just as it has been the goal of previous therapies to recover the repressed contents of the unconscious, so the goal of ecopsychology is to awaken the inherent sense of environmental reciprocity that lies within the ecological unconscious. Other therapies seek to heal the alienation between person and person, person and family, person and society. Ecopsychology seeks to heal the more fundamental alienation between the person and the natural environment.
>
> (Roszak 1992: 320)

Human development and nature

By taking an evolutionary perspective on human–nature relationships, Shepard (1982) attempts to historicise aspects of how humans have become disconnected from nature. He sees a form of ontogenetic crippling as evolving with the birth of agriculture – a crucial point at which he believes humans created a false sense of separation from the natural habitat. Recent writing by authors such as Louv (2008) has posited the idea of 'Nature Deficit Disorder', aping criteria from psychiatric diagnosis, to argue that children are suffering from a deficit of contact with the natural world. A recent campaign by the Royal Society for the Protection of Birds in the UK looking at children's connection to nature, based on a questionnaire measure developed by Cheng and Monroe (2012), found that just one in five children in the UK felt connected to nature.

Searles (1960) proposed that although essential psychodynamic concepts were contained within Freud's writings, he failed, as have subsequent others since, to explicitly acknowledge the significance of the non-human environment in the development of human psychological life. Searles raises the importance in infant development of the relationship with both the mother and what Searles terms the 'non-human environment':

> the human being is engaged, throughout his lifespan, in an unceasing struggle to differentiate himself increasingly fully, not only from his human, but also from his non-human environment, while developing, in proportion as he succeeds in these differentiations, an increasingly meaningful relatedness with the latter environment as well as with his fellow human beings.
>
> (1960: 30)

Barrows (1995) argues that a new theory of child development must be evolved, taking into consideration that the infant is born into not only a social but an ecological context. It seems that counselling and psychotherapy need to consider a more complex way of understanding development and life as embedded in multifaceted environments, both human and non-human, and that this is linked to understanding and treating emotional and psychological distress. Developing this further, some forms of psychotherapeutic intervention, most notably ecotherapy as the applied practice of ecopsychology, see reconnective ecological communication, i.e. fostering a reciprocal relationship between person and planet, as the central focus of counselling and psychotherapy.

Reconnective ecological communication

The idea that we can 'reconnect' to something we have lost in terms of our ability to communicate ecologically is a dominant theme in several writings in the area of ecopsychology, and ecotherapy in particular (Buzzell and Chalquist 2009). It seems to strongly suggest that a pre-modern world with a pure and reciprocal ecological communication with nature and the non-human has been lost or disrupted. The idea and image of indigenous peoples living a way of life that is in connection with the natural world becomes an ideal for ecopsychology and positing an ecological self (Roszak et al. 1995).

The ideas underpinning reconnectivity can be traced back to the Romantic Movement. As a reaction to the industrial revolution and the rationalism of the Enlightenment, the Romantic Movement as espoused by writers such as Wordsworth sought to offer an antidote to what was perceived as the deadening effect of modernity (Bate 1991). Drawing from these ideas, either implicitly or explicitly, ecopsychology has argued that modernity and industrialisation have had a deadening effect on the self and a destructive effect on the natural world.

Jung (1989) was convinced that the earth is sentient, a living entity, stating that we are not only upon the world but the earth is within us. Along with many others,

Jung struggled to find the language to express this connection because of its subtlety. Crediting the idea to Lévy-Bruhl (1921/1926), Jung (1921/1971) uses the term 'participation mystique' to describe how indigenous peoples do not distinguish themselves sharply from the environment, believing that what went on outside also went on inside of the self, as captured in much mythology. Tacey (2009) picks up Jung's ideas in discussing the 'sacred' nature of the earth, identifying three stages in the trajectory of the mind's disconnection and reconnection to nature. The first stage Tacey suggests is pre-modern literalism and supernaturalism, the belief that there are spirits of the earth in the form of forces which require the mediation of shamans and priests. This animistic stage has been represented by modernity as irrational and anthropomorphic, the projections of an irrational mind seeking to understand the mechanisms of the earth that have been thoroughly worked out by the scientific processes of modernity. The second stage, which I will call modernity, and Tacey refers to as modern disbelief and scepticism, sees the animistic paganism of the pre-modern systems of ecological communication as arising from disturbed infantile, unenlightened minds. The last stage in the disconnection from the earth is an attempt at reconnection in the form of the 'post-rational vision'. This stage, argues Tacey, is the most difficult to achieve as we need to move on from our modernist scientific roots which dominate the way we perceive nature. It involves a re-evaluation of fantasy, imagination and projection, sorting out the personal from the archetypical, the idea that 'land' in its vibrancy may be affecting us in all sorts of ways that we are unable to articulate.

The idea of 'nature' as animate, containing transpersonal forces mediated through reconnective practices which break down the duality of mind and nature, can be seen in particular forms of therapeutic process in nature. The work of Foster and Little (1983, 1989, 1992, 1998) focuses on the process of the vision quest as a mechanism of psychological change. Their work draws from rites of passage models known to traditional cultures as ways of negotiating life stages (Van Gennep 1960). The modern-day vision quest advocated by Foster and Little (1983) places the individual within a wilderness environment without food or shelter for a solitary three- or four-day experience of aloneness. This experience is then shared with others in a group process in order to make meaning and gain a 'vision' or life purpose that is contextualised as part of a process of transition for that individual. I participated in an experience such as this (Jordan 2005) and suffered from a profound depression subsequent to returning from the process. One of the main problems is the cultural context within which this form of experience and process is understood. Something which made sense to the plains Native Americans (Black Elk 1972) does not contextualise within a late modern culture. Remembering one's connection to the natural world as essential to 'coming home', does not easily translate to contemporary urban life. For me, any therapeutic experience in 'nature' needs to be movement between different spaces of an individual's life, not a jarring dislocation between one extreme and another, the urban and the wilderness environment, in the hope of returning to a pre-modern fantasy of ecological communication. At worst some of these experiences are no more than a psychological one-night stand with nature, not properly contextualised and situated within a person's life and cultural framework. However, the need to set up reconnective process with natural phenomena is arguably vital to both emotional and mental well-being and forms a strong thread within reconnective ideas and practice.

Writers such as Metzner (1995) argue that we need to recover our ancestors' capacity to empathise and identify with non-human life, using ancient traditions of initiation and ritual celebration to develop an ecological literacy. What Metzner points to represents a strong strand in ecopsychological thought and practice, the sense of reconnection to something lost, with the pre-modern being the place where this perfect connection and reciprocity existed between the natural world and humans, and what we need to recover. A particular form of ecological connection is advocated which suggests a strong pull to move backwards to a pre-modern form of ecological communication with the natural.

The ecological connection to the earth in the form of reconnective and transpersonal practice points towards one of the central challenges of ecological communication: that contact with nature feels real and is experienced on several different levels concurrently, yet when we seek to articulate it, 'it' can remain elusive. Tacey (2009: 49) says it can be 'felt but not reasoned' and points us towards the nature–mind–experience connection that remains quite elusive if we have to rely solely on thought, language and reason to explain its affect. The problem is in attempting to use a modern mindset to both explain and articulate this connection. We are in danger of romanticising the pre-modern (as seen in films such as *Avatar*: Cameron 2009), seeking reconnection to something we have fundamentally lost and are hoping to recover. It seems to reduce the possibility of forms of ecological communication more suited to and understood in late modernity.

Human–nature relationships – what is nature?

Before we can begin to explore the practice and process of counselling and psychotherapy in natural spaces, we have to examine how the natural environment was separated from psyche (and culture) in the first place. It is important to understand how we have positioned ourselves as beings with interiors who view exteriors, and how these exteriors were positioned as something extrinsic to the selves who viewed them. This position for the psyche has fundamental implications for theories of counselling and psychotherapy and in some sense forces us to re-imagine what therapeutic practice and process would look like when we move outdoors. From my review of the literature on nature-based therapies (outlined in Chapter 2), quite often the question of what actually constitutes nature is ignored or touched upon without a deeper engagement with some of the philosophical and psychological problems that arise in addressing the question.

The first problem is how the natural environment is understood and defined. My definition takes into account the context of where counselling and psychotherapy, as it is practised by therapists, might take place. These are: nearby nature (Kaplan and Kaplan 1989) and more remote nature in the form of wilderness (Macfarlane 2007; Marris 2011). However it is important to note that the concepts of 'nature' and 'wilderness' are quite problematic and our understanding of these concepts has shifted throughout history, especially in relation to culture and technological development. Recent writing contests the idea of nature as a uniform concept, stating that it is impossible to situate it as a singular entity (Macnaghten and Urry 1998). Nature has emerged historically through its articulation in the natural sciences (Latour 1993) and through the practices and economic developments of modernity (Bluhdorn 2001).

Soper (1995) says that the concept and use of the word 'nature' have become ubiquitous and it is employed with such ease and regularity that it defies definition. However, nature has also become a vehicle through which various ideologies and paradigms are at work and in conflict with one another. Soper (1995) says that in recent times it has come to occupy a political place as a result of the ecological crisis, becoming a concept through which we are asked to re-think the use of resources, relationships to other life forms and our place and responsibilities within a wider ecosystem. Nature exists between the discourses of ecology and recent theory in cultural and critical studies. Soper says that this distinction is not neat and clear, in that it is both subject and object and the two are not easily negotiated and separated, quite often overlapping and folding back onto one another.

Taking a postmodern approach to understanding nature, Anderson (2009) defines it as an 'emerging postnature'. Following from Latour (1993) and Whatmore (1999), Anderson states there has never been an ontological separation between humans and nature, that the idea of 'pure' nature outside of society is a fallacy. He argues that, in a world of merging and emerging ontologies, the concepts of nature, culture and mind can never really be positioned as distinct entities, separate from one another. The world and those who move within it all change over time, both immersed in one another and emergent at the same time. In these merging and emerging movements we do not find a distinct 'mind' coming into contact with a distinct 'nature' through a distinct 'culture'. Anderson goes on to say that:

> Postnature is therefore not simply a locking together of separate entities within a passive context rather it is a convergence of mutual interaction and interference involving humans, non-humans and place. The meaning of any human or non-human species in this assemblage can thus only be marginally known if taken in isolation.
>
> (2009: 123)

As nature and human minds have traditionally been separated, how do we resist the urge to constantly split the world into binary forms in order to deal with its otherness, to negotiate the interior and exterior domains? There is an inevitability to the dualities that we create through thought and feeling that lead to action and the development of cultural forms and representations of nature and the environment. How do we find the space in between? Morton offers us *The Ecological*

Thought (Morton 2010), where reality is devoid of reified, rigid, or conceptual notions of subject and object, inside and out, so that we exist in an infinite web of mutual interdependence where there is no boundary or centre (Morton 2007: 23). Indeed, says Morton, all this conceptual boundary making is part of the problem.

I have proposed elsewhere (Jordan 2012) that arguing for a unified self in relation to a unified nature is perhaps illusory given the time we live in, and instead would support an argument for an emerging 'post-nature' (Anderson 2009) and a more distributed and disrupted self. I much prefer the term 'natural space' to nature, because the term natural space denotes that there are different spaces, some containing a greater volume of natural processes and materials, e.g. forests and mountains, and some containing both natural and man-made features such as local parks and woodlands. None the less there are some real issues to be engaged with in counselling and psychotherapy in relation to the environmental crisis, and a therapeutic rationale driven by these concerns needs to be carefully thought out.

The danger in taking a postmodern approach to the question of what is nature is that issues in relation to the material aspects of nature and its physicality potentially get lost alongside a deeper and more profound understanding of the force driving nature, growth and evolution. Nature is not just a 'text'; there is something corporeal and material that needs to be accounted for and understood as part of the complex relationships between humans and nature in a post-natural world. Next I outline certain philosophical strands in order to understand nature as both material and semiotic, concrete and yet a process, vibrant and vital in its capacity to affect the humans who interact with it.

Nature as a process of becoming

Philosophies of becoming are linked to the ideas of process philosopher A. N. Whitehead and the geophilosophies of Deleuze and Guattari (1988, 1994), and more recent attempts to find common ground between these theorists in the form of 'becoming' (Faber and Stephenson 2011; Connolly 2011). Both offer a way to re-imagine human–nature relationships as movement and immanent unfolding. This allows us to move beyond the position favoured by Cartesian-influenced thinking of a separate mind and a separate nature, which leads us down a path of binary dualities. These spaces of subject and object are at once both material and subjective, semiotic and objective. Philosophies of becoming allow us to challenge the idea of subjectivity and nature as fixed locations somehow separate from one another which need to be re-joined in order to form an ecological self. For those of us who find ourselves at this time in history, the notion of subjectivity and nature as fixed points does not capture the spatiotemporal flux of both of these positions within modernity, postmodernity and globalisation. Climate change positions us in a complex web of global inter-relationships, which are biotic, political, scientific, subjective and above all emotional and psychological. An ecological subject has to find their bearings amongst all of these complex flows and relations.

Whitehead's process philosophical position (1920/2004, 1978) presents a relational theory of matter, where the 'object' observed is the attributes it possesses in relation to space. Whitehead (1920/2004) proposes a revision of the subject–object split into a process philosophy that sees things as existing in relationships within particular forms, which in themselves are context-dependent on the perspective of the viewer and relationships between attributes of substances, spaces and times. Thus his philosophy is a process theory of relationships between entities in time and space, viewed from the interpretive stance of the observer.

> Accordingly it would seem that every material entity is not really one entity. It is an essential multiplicity of entities. There seems to be no stopping this dissociation of matter into multiplicities short of finding each ultimate entity occupying one individual point.
>
> (Whitehead 1920/2004: 22)

Sense awareness becomes important in our relations to nature; this is an area both independent of, and related to, thoughts about nature. Whitehead believes our sense perception about nature is disclosed as a complex set of entities whose mutual relations are expressible in the heterogeneity of thought and sense awareness. For Whitehead there is a problem of homogeneity in our relations with nature, which through our doctrines of science have caused a bifurcation of nature and mind. Nature is a 'complex of fact', a heterogeneous experience of 'events' in motion. Whitehead (1978) calls these events in motion 'actual occasions', in that there is nothing behind things to make them more real; their reality comes through in the process of the becoming of actual occasions. In this sense nature loses its static material quality as positioned by dominant modes of scientific thought. Isaac Newton, argues Whitehead, fell into the 'fallacy of misplaced concreteness'. So the physical world becomes bound together not by laws, which Whitehead argues are not always followed clearly anyway, but by a general type of relatedness, a process of becoming, rather than the concrete end point positioned as material reality.

Vitalism: the position of matter and materiality in mind–nature communication

As a concept, vitalism originated in the eighteenth and nineteenth centuries (Fraser et al. 2005). Its central premise was that life cannot be explained by the mechanistic processes advocated in certain forms of scientific and biological theorising, in particular Darwinian, Newtonian and Cartesian. Calkins (1919) outlines some of the fundamental differences between mechanism and vitalism. Mechanism, she argues, describes the universe in structural terms; vitalism in contrast explains the universe in terms of relations. Because of its emphasis on structure and function, mechanism is deterministic, whereas vitalism conceives of an incalculable and unpredictable controlling force or entelechy, moving the organism to some sense of fulfilment. In applying vitalistic ideas to psychology, Calkins challenges the mind as purely material and mechanistic; rather being psychologically vitalistic, it is fundamentally personalistic and understands the universe in terms of relational processes and is conscious in these terms. Consciousness of nature comes in the form of a personal relationship not solely reducible to materiality or mechanistic cause and effect processes.

Hans Driesch's original classic on vitalism, *The History and Theory of Vitalism* (1914), discusses some of the central premises of vitalism, the idea that life has a purposive or teleological drive. Driesch sees a special kind of teleology at work within the realm of organic life, that there is some underlying driving force in things. In viewing life in purely mechanistic and material terms we are led through what Driesch refers to as 'static' or 'descriptive' forms of teleology, leaving us with the question of an un-analysable autonomy. As a solution, Driesch proposes a dynamic teleology; foregrounding the notion of a vital entelechy; we are led to a doctrine of real organic 'becoming'. Driesch states that vitalism explains the essential difference of the 'life' machine which appears as something different from the technical machine. Life is a series of relations moving forwards in an unfolding process of becoming, driven by a life force, which is not reducible to mechanistic or purely material explanations.

Vitalism as a theory became deeply unfashionable and discredited, with mechanistic and material explanations dominating the understanding and explanations of organic matter and the way it functioned. But vitalism has re-emerged in the social sciences in recent decades, driven by a concern to understand ideas such as complexity and uncertainty, the hybridity between organic and machine and the evolving processes of information technology and the world wide web. Lash (2006) says the notion of 'life' has always favoured 'becoming' over just 'being', action over structure, the flow and flux. Vitalism, Lash argues, always presumes an emergent form. In the return to vitalism as an underpinning idea used to explain life, the senses become important, an experiencing based on a sensate connection as a form of knowing. This can especially be seen in David Abram's book, *The Spell of the Sensuous*, narrating the author's sensate connection to nature, and other forms of nature writing (Abram 1996).

Colebrook (2010) says that systems designed to enhance life, such as modern medicine, can often develop into alienating and monstrous forms, e.g. rats with human ears growing on them in order to aid medical advancement. This leaves us feeling alienated and deadened, cut off from our feelings and senses. Colebrook proposes that vitalism as an idea is appealing because it is overwhelmingly organic and committed to a deeper sense of evolving meaning and purpose.

Another recent writer, Bennet (2004), has advocated a contemporary form of vitalism, proposing that we can account for matter in terms of the affect it has on humans, what she terms 'thing power'. Rather than a dead material space, things acquire power in terms of their ability to hold matter and energy in the spaces between inert matter and vital energy, between animate and inanimate 'and where all things to some degree live on both sides' (Bennet 2004: 352). Bennet (2010) uses assemblage theory to explore the heterogeneous assemblages where humans and things interweave and assemble one another. This one-substance doctrine allows us to dissolve the Cartesian legacy of mind independent of nature; the entire universe is conceived of as a single space-time entity, which rather than being composed of discrete parts gives rise to fields which are located within it (Garret 2001). The idea that the material world is not separate from those who inhabit it, both linked together in an unfolding, interdependent relational process, has been picked up in philosophy. Here we can see where several strands of thought both in academia and beyond have been attempting to articulate how forms of mind–nature relations intrinsically shape one another.

Vitalism and geophilosophy

Geophilosophy is a position within philosophy that advocates that thought and earth are intertwined (Bonta and Protevi 2004). The idea of a geophilosophical position, a philosophy that relates to and is formed by the earth, can be traced back to the writings of Deleuze and Guattari (1988, 1994). Deleuze and Guattari's writings have been notoriously difficult to understand and decipher, precisely because they attempt to undermine facets of a concrete material reality as it has been previously represented in much natural and social scientific writing. They challenge notions of representation, instead arguing for production, rather than a transcendent reality where we can sit above concepts, and draw from stable theoretical groundings. They argue for immanence, and their emphasis is on emergent co-involved materiality and subjectivity (Herzogenrath 2009). Their ideas are not merely clever linguistic musings and metaphorical locations, rather they are an attempt to fully locate thought and earth in intertwined processes of becoming. They are important for re-imagining the reciprocal relation between humans and nature because of their emphasis on 'affect', in that an individual entity, be it a subject or a rock, can affect and be affected by other individual entities (DeLanda 2006). Chisholm (2007) proposes that Deleuze and Guattari in *A Thousand Plateaus* move us toward Bateson's ideas of an 'ecology of mind' (Bateson 2000). She argues that they are moving us away from philosophical notions of the transcendental, ideas that are deduced above the contingencies of the terrain of the earth. One of the central ideas of immanence is that it is contingent upon the complex processes of earthly life, entirely dependent on the self-ordering capacities of complex systems, not an extra-worldly source such as God (Chisholm 2007; Bonta and Protevi 2004).

The rhizome (Deleuze and Guattari 1988) is a way of helping understand two central themes of their project: the notion of multiplicity and that of heterogeneous thought. The rhizome is a concept taken directly from biology. Unlike tap roots which form trees and branches, what Deleuze and Guattari call 'arborescent thought', the rhizome is a subterranean structure which connects every point to every other point:

it is composed not of units but of dimensions, or rather directions in motion. It has neither beginning nor end, but always a middle (milieu) from which it grows and overspills. It constitutes linear multiplicities with dimensions having neither subject nor object, which can be laid out on a plain of consistency . . . Unlike a structure, which is defined by a set of points and positions, with binary relations between the points and biunivocal relationships between positions, the rhizome is made of only lines: lines of segmentarity and stratification as its dimensions, and the line of flight or deterritorialisation as the maximum dimension after which the multiplicity undergoes metamorphosis, changes in nature.

(1988: 27)

In this sense we can see how thought is located in spaces, and becomes linked to the earth, not via branch-like (linear) thought structures, but via points in a rhizomatic assemblage. Deleuze and Guattari argue that systems of thinking which are linked to Cartesian and Newtonian thought, and which posit a concrete reality, are caught in an arboreal trap, locating subjects and objects, interiors and exteriors, within fixed tree-like locations. The intertwined conceptual and biological processes of the rhizome represent an understanding of the multiplicity. Within the Deleuze and Guattari notion of becoming (Delueze and Guattari 1988) we are always arriving, never fully settling. In this sense a critique of process ideas could argue that in this way of thinking we are unable to stop in order to be able to see anything stable and this can be quite unnerving.

In re-imagining the importance of the natural world for the human psyche and the potential for its therapeutic use in counselling and psychotherapy we need to deal with issues of the materiality of the outside natural world and its relationship to human subjectivity. Rather than positioning 'nature' as only discursively constructed, a danger of postmodern relativism, we have to make a methodological space that will enable us to think about humans and nature as co-existent and interdependent, mergent and emergent in relational processes.

Forms of vitalism in psychotherapy

This section concludes by considering recent writing in psychotherapy which has foregrounded the notion of vitality as important to mental health and well-being. Daniel Stern, who has written some seminal texts on the importance of developing sense of self through infant development and its relationship to psychotherapy (Stern 1985), has recently written on the centrality of forms of vitality to infant development and psychotherapy. Stern (2010) defines vitality as a manifestation of being alive and essential to human experience, something distinct from known physical, chemical and mental forces. Drawing from the original ideas of vitalism as a dynamic teleology, a moving unfolding and relational force of becoming, vitality is positioned as a constant sense of movement which maintains our sense of being alive. Rather than forms of internal mental representation driving action and thought, action is based on feeling states, sensate connections of relations, and a dynamic unfolding of relationships between internal and external, between humans and the wider world around them (Ingold 2011). Stern (2010) proposes that dynamic forms of vitality provide a path for psychotherapy to access non-conscious past experience, including memories, dissociated experiences, phenomenological experience, past implicit experience never verbalised, and what he terms 'implicit relational knowing' – how we implicitly know how 'to be with' a specific other. Stern talks about our dynamic movement signature, the way we walk, talk, reach for things, all unique forms of individual vitality which have evolved from the general to the specific, in the moment-to-moment process of adaption and enactment. These vitality dynamics are crucial for the living organism to fit within its environment. Movement is important to our experience and is a primary and fundamental aspect of our animate evolution both individually and as a species. It is of course embodied but also arises out of other forms of dynamic movement, such as music as 'sound in motion', reading and hearing language, visual stimuli such as art and film, all of which we can experience as virtual worlds of forces in motion (Stern 2010: 20).

Stern makes a link to Gestalt thinking, seeing vital forms as a whole, rather than as separate entities. These are overarching terms which challenge the mechanistic reductionism of certain forms of psychological understanding. He also links vitalism to neuroscientific thinking, in particular theorising about the role of the arousal system which has a crucial role in the formation of unreflected dynamic experience. Stern makes a link to the arousal system and vitality, seeing arousal as a 'fundamental force' for all bodily and mental activity contained within the central nervous system. Stern links forms of vitality found in forms of music, dance, theatre and cinema to our arousal systems, which have an effect on us from moment to moment when listening to music, or over longer stretches of time, for example when watching a film.

Interestingly Stern makes no reference to nature as a form of vitality operating upon human arousal systems, but it is not too great a link to include nature in his forms of vitality as it contains elements which would affect arousal systems through visual, sensory and bodily states. We might also hypothesise about 'affect attunement' to natural spaces and link this to Ulrich's ideas about a psychoevolutionary connection with natural environments and stress reduction, and also to research coming from Japan about the effect of immersions in the forest on cortisol systems (Tsunetsugu et al. 2007).

In conclusion, Stern sees vitality forms as essential forms of interpersonal happenings: the infant needs much dynamic information to recognise how some-one moves, gets angry or when and how the focus of their attention is directed; experience for the infant is multisensory. As mentioned previously, Shepard (1982) and Barrows (1995) have articulated the importance of sensate connection to nature in this process and its links to mental health. Louv (2008) also makes a similar point about the effects of a deficit of contact with nature in children. Stern's forms of vitality allow us to see the important clinical links for therapy about why contact with nature is essential and how this links to vital processes of arousal within infants and adults as they grow.

Concluding comments

There is considerable evidence which supports the positive psychological and healing effects of nature upon the psyche. The growth of 'green care' over the last fifteen years is indicative of an emerging movement seeking to place our contact and engagement with nature as central to improved mental health. The growth in the importance of nature to well-being has given rise to the emergence of a new discipline: ecopsychology. Ecopsychology has been central in supporting ideas within counselling and psychotherapy which position nature as fundamental to revitalising and reconnecting humans within a reciprocal healing relationship to nature. In this chapter I have also outlined a philosophical position for nature which links it intrinsically to our minds and our sense of aliveness. This is important for understanding nature's role in revitalising therapeutic space and psychotherapeutic process.

References

Abram, D. (1996) *The Spell of the Sensuous: Perception and Language in a More-than-Human World.* New York: Vintage.

Anderson, J. (2009) Transient convergence and relational sensibility: beyond the modern constitution of nature. *Emotion, Space and Society* 2, 120–127.

Barrows, A. (1995) The ecopsychology of child development. In T. Roszak, M. Gomes and A. Kanner (eds) *Ecopsychology: Restoring the Earth, Healing the Mind.* London: Sierra Club.

Bate, J. (1991) *Romantic Ecology: Wordsworth and the Environmental Tradition.* London: Routledge.

Bateson, G. (1972) *Steps to an Ecology of Mind: Collected Essays in Anthropology, Psychiatry, Evolution and Epistemology.* New York: Ballantine.

Bateson, G. (2000) *Steps to an Ecology of Mind: Collected Essays in Anthropology, Psychiatry, Evolution, and Epistemology*, new edn. Chicago: University of Chicago Press.

Bennet, J. (2004) The force of things: steps toward an ecology of matter. *Political Theory* 32(3), 347–372.

Bennet, J. (2010) *Vibrant Matter: A Political Ecology of Things.* Durham, NC: Duke University Press.

Black Elk (1972) *Black Elk Speaks: Being the Life Story of a Holy Man of the Oglala Sioux/ as Told through John G. Neihardt (Flaming Rainbow).* London: Barrie Jenkins.

Bluhdorn, I. (2001) Reflexivity and self-referentiality: on the normative foundations of ecological communication. In C. B. Grant and D. McLaughlin (eds) *Language-Meaning-Social Construction Interdisciplinary Studies.* New York: Rodopi, pp. 181–201.

Bonta, M. and Protevi, J. (2004) *Deleuze and Geophilosophy: A Guide and a Glossary.* Edinburgh: Edinburgh University Press.

Boston, T. (1996) Ecopsychology: an earth-psyche bond. *Trumpeter* 13(2) http:///trumpeter. athabascau.ca/index.php/trumpet/article/viewArticle/269/402 (accessed 10 July 2007).

Buzzell, L and Chalquist, C. (2009) *Ecotherapy: Healing with Nature in Mind*. San Francisco: Sierra Club.

Calkins, M. W. (1919) The personalistic conception of nature. *The Philosophical Review* 28(2), 115–146.

Cameron (2009) *Avatar* (distributed by 20th Century Fox).

Cheng, J. C. and Munroe, M. C. (2012) Connection to nature: children's affective attitude toward nature. *Environment and Behaviour* 44(1), 31–49.

Chisholm, D. (2007) Rhizome, ecology, geophilosophy (a map to this issue). *Rhizomes* 15(winter). www.rhizomes.net/issue15/chisholm.html (accessed 20/10/2010).

Clayton, S. and Myers, G. (2009) *Conservation Psychology: Understanding and Promoting Human Care for Nature*. London: Wiley.

Colebrook, C. (2010) *Deleuze and the Meaning of Life*. London: Continuum.

Connolly, W. E. (2011) *A World of Becoming*. Durham, NC: Duke University Press.

Deakin, R. (2008) Call of the wild. *Guardian Weekend*, 25 October.

DeLanda, M. (2006) *A New Philosophy of Society: Assemblage Theory and Social Complexity*. London: Continuum.

Deleuze, G. and Guattari, F. (1988) *A Thousand Plateaus: Capitalism and Schizophrenia*. Trans. B. Massumi. London: Continuum.

Deleuze, G. and Guattari, F. (1994) *What Is Philosophy?* Trans. G. Burchell and H. Tomlinson. London: Verso.

Downie, R. S., Tannahill, C. and Tannahill, A. (2000) *Health Promotion Models and Values*, 2nd edn. Oxford: Oxford University Press.

Driesch, H. (1914) *The History and Theory of Vitalism*. Trans. C. K. Ogden. London: Macmillan and Co.

Faber, R. and Stephenson, A. M. (eds) (2011) *Secrets of Becoming: Negotiating Whitehead, Deleuze, and Butler*. New York: Fordham University Press.

Foster, S. and Little, M. (1983) *The Trail to the Sacred Mountain: A Vision Fast Handbook for Adults*. Big Pine, CA: Lost Borders Press.

Foster, S. and Little, M. (1989) *The Roaring of The Sacred River: The Wilderness Quest for Vision and Self Healing*. Big Pine. CA: Lost Borders Press.

Foster, S. and Little, M. (1992) *The Book of The Vision Quest: Personal Transformation in The Wilderness*. New York: Fireside Books.

Foster, S. and Little, M. (1998) *The Four Shields: The Initiatory Seasons of Human Nature*. Big Pine, CA: Lost Borders Press.

Fraser, M., Kember, S. and Lury, C. (2005) Inventive life: approaches to the new vitalism. *Theory, Culture and Society* 22(1), 1–14.

Frumkin, H. (2012) Building the science base: ecopsychology meets clinical epidemiology. In P. H. Kahn and P. H. Hasbach (eds) *Ecopsychology: Science, Totems and the Technological Species*. Cambridge, MA: MIT Press.

Garret, D. (2001) Introduction. In B. Spinoza, *Ethics*. Trans. W. H. White, rev. A. H. Sterling. Ware: Wordsworth Editions.

Greenway, R. (2010) What is ecopsychology? *Gatherings Journal* www.ecopsychology. org/journal/gatherings/what.htm (accessed 27 May 2010).

Herzogenrath, B. (ed.) (2009) *Deleuze/Guattari and Ecology*. London: Palgrave Macmillan.

Hillman, J. (1975) *Re-Visioning Psychology*. London: HarperCollins.

Ingold, T. (2011) *Being Alive: Essays on Movement Knowledge and Description*. London: Routledge.

Jordan, M. (2005) The vision quest: a transpersonal process. Paper presented to the British Psychological Society Transpersonal Psychology Section Conference, 17 September 2005.

Jordan, M. (2012) Did Lacan go camping? Psychotherapy in search of an ecological self. In M. J. Rust and N. Totton (eds) *Vital Signs: Psychological Responses to the Ecological Crisis.* London: Karnac.

Jung, C. G. (1921/1971). *Psychological Types. Collected Works*, vol. 6. Princeton, NJ: Princeton University Press.

Jung, C. G. (1989) *Memories, Dreams and Reflections.* New York: Knopf.

Kaplan, R. and Kaplan, S. (1989) *The Experience of Nature: A Psychological Perspective.* Cambridge: Cambridge University Press.

Kaplan, S. (1995) The restorative benefits of nature: towards an integrative framework. *Journal of Environmental Psychology* 16, 169–182.

Kellert, S. (1993) The Biophilia Hypothesis. In Stephen R. Kellert and Edward O. Wilson (eds) *The Biophilia Hypothesis.* Washington, DC: Island Press.

Kidner, D. (2007) Depression and the natural world: towards a critical ecology of distress. *Critical Psychology* 19, 123–146.

Lash, S. (2006) Life (vitalism). *Theory, Culture and Society* 23(2–3), 323–349.

Latour, R. (1993) *We Have Never Been Modern.* Hemel Hempstead: Harvester Wheatsheaf.

Lee, J., Park, B. J., Tsunetsugu, Y., Kagawa, T. and Miyazaki, Y. (2011) Physiological benefits of forest environment: based on field research at 4 sites. *Nihon Eiseigaku Zasshi* 66(4), 663–669.

Lévy-Bruhl, L. (1912/1926). *How Natives Think.* Trans. Lilian A. Clare. London: George Allen & Unwin.

Louv, R. (2008) *Last Child in the Woods: Saving Our Children from Nature Deficit Disorder.* Chapel Hill, NC: Algonquin Books.

Macfarlane, R. (2007) *The Wild Places.* London: Granta.

Macnaghten, P. and Urry, J. (1998) *Contested Natures.* London: Sage.

Macy, J. (2007) *World as Lover: World as Self.* London: Parallax Press.

Marris, E. (2011) *Rambunctious Garden: Saving Nature in a Post-Wild World.* London: Bloomsbury.

Metzner, R. (1995) The psychopathology of the human nature relationship. In T. Roszak, A. Kanner and M. Gomes (eds) *Ecopsychology: Restoring the Earth and Healing the Mind.* London: Sierra Club Books.

Morton, T. (2007) *Ecology without Nature: Rethinking Environmental Ethics.* Cambridge, MA: Harvard University Press.

Morton, T. (2010) *The Ecological Thought.* Cambridge, MA: Harvard University Press.

Naess, A. (1973) The shallow and the deep, long range ecology movement. A summary. *Inquiry* 16, 95–100.

Reser, J. (1995) Whither environmental psychology? The transpersonal ecopsychology crossroads. *Journal of Environmental Psychology* 15(3), 235–257.

Roszak, T. (1992) *The Voice of the Earth.* London: Simon & Schuster.

Roszak, T., Gomes, M. and Kanner, A. (1995) *Ecopsychology: Restoring the Earth, Healing the Mind.* London: Sierra Club.

Schroll, M. (2007) Wrestling with Arne Naess: a chronicle of ecopsychology's origins. *Trumpeter* 23(1), 28–57.

Scull, J. (2009) Ecopsychology: where does it fit in psychology in 2009? *Trumpeter* 24(3), 68–85.

Searles, H. (1960) *The Nonhuman Environment: In Normal Development and in Schizophrenia.* New York: International Universities Press.

Seed, J., Macy, J., Fleming, P. and Naess, A. (1993) *Thinking Like a Mountain: Towards a Council of All Beings.* London: New Society.

Selhub, E. M. and Logan, A. (2012) *Your Brain on Nature: The Science of Nature's Influence on Your Health, Happiness, and Vitality.* Ontario: Wiley.

Sempik, J., Hine, R. and Wilcox, D. (eds) (2010) *Green Care: A Conceptual Framework, A Report of the Working Group on the Health Benefits of Green Care, COST Action 866, Green Care in Agriculture.* Loughborough: Centre for Child and Family Research, Loughborough University.

Shepard, P. (1982) *Nature and Madness.* San Francisco: Sierra Club Books.

Shepard, P. (1995) Nature and madness. In T. Roszak, A. Kanner and M. Gomes (eds) *Ecopsychology: Restoring the Earth and Healing the Mind.* London: Sierra Club Books.

Soper, K. (1995) *What Is Nature?* London: Blackwell.

Stern, D. (1985) *The Interpersonal World of the Infant: A View from Psychoanalysis and Developmental Psychology.* New York: Basic Books.

Stern, D. N. (2010) *Forms of Vitality: Exploring Dynamic Experience in Psychology, the Arts, Psychotherapy, and Development.* Oxford: Oxford University Press.

Stigsdotter, U. and Grahn, P. (2003) Experiencing a garden: a healing garden for people suffering from burnout diseases. *Journal of Therapeutic Horticulture* XIV, 39–49.

Tacey, D. (2009) *The Edge of Sacred: Jung, Psyche, Earth.* Einsiedeln, Switzerland: Daimon Verlag.

Tsunetsugu, Y., Park, B. J., Ishii, H., Hirano, H., Kagawa, T. and Miyazaki, Y. (2007) Physiological effects of Shinrin-yoku (taking in the atmosphere of the forest) in an old-growth broadleaf forest in Yamagata Prefecture, Japan. *Journal of Physiological Anthropology* 26(2), 135–142.

Ulrich, R. S. (1983) Aesthetic and affective response to natural environment. In I. Altman and J. F. Wohill (eds) *Behaviour and the Natural Environment.* New York: Plenum Press.

Ulrich, R. (1984) View through a window may influence recovery from surgery. *Science* 224, 420–421.

Van Gennep, A. (1960) *The Rites of Passage.* Chicago: University of Chicago Press.

Whatmore, S. (1999) Nature culture. In P. Cloke, M. Crang and M. Goodwin (eds) *Introducing Human Geographies.* London: Arnold.

Whitehead, A. N. (1920/2004) *The Concept of Nature.* New York: Prometheus.

Whitehead, A. N. (1978) *Process and Reality*, corrected edition. Ed. David R. Griffin and Donald W. Sherburne. New York: Free Press.

Wilson, E. O. (1984) *Biophilia: The Human Bond with Other Species.* Cambridge, MA: Harvard University Press.

Chapter 2

The field of nature-based therapies

There is no one overarching definition of outdoor therapy, or a comprehensive model in terms of how to practise therapy in outdoor natural spaces. Over a number of years a 'field' of practice has developed in taking therapeutic work into the outdoors. Some of this field has had a long history, particularly in the United States in the form of adventure and wilderness therapy, and I will review aspects of this literature in terms of how theory and practice are understood. There have also been more recent developments in the form of nature therapy and ecotherapy, which draw upon ideas from ecopsychology (Roszak et al. 1995). Ecopsychology attempts to develop epistemological arguments around the nature of self and relationships to nature which have largely been ignored or under-theorised in psychology. It is these ideas which inform aspects of ecotherapy (Buzzell and Chalquist 2009) and some versions of counselling and psychotherapy in natural environments.

The most written about form of therapy in the outdoors is adventure therapy (Richards and Peel 2005; Gass et al. 2012). However a plethora of terms exist which attempt to articulate what therapeutic practice in the outdoors might be: wilderness therapy (Berman and Berman 1994), ecotherapy (Clinebell 1996; MIND 2007), nature therapy (Berger 2007), nature-guided therapy (Burns 1998), relational therapy in the outdoors (Santostefano 2004). There is a lot of work that defines itself as therapeutic but is not clearly counselling or psychotherapy as I would understand it, and so in reviewing the literature I will critically question what clearly has a grounding in counselling and psychotherapy practice and ideas.

I will initially outline three main approaches which have some grounding in counselling and psychotherapy and which will point the way forward in terms of what has already been articulated about therapeutic practice outdoors and some of the gaps that this book will attempt to address. In particular I want to address issues in understanding therapeutic practice outdoors, for example how to hold a therapeutic frame outdoors and different aspects of therapeutic process and relationship as they apply to counselling and psychotherapy outdoors.

The natural growth project – psychotherapy within a gardening context

The natural growth project represents a comprehensive attempt to write about the process of conducting psychotherapy in natural contexts, in particular within allotments and gardens. In attempting to write about the project, Jenny Grut (Linden and Grut 2002) stated that even after ten years of working with the victims of torture in nature it was very difficult to articulate the subtle healing effects of nature upon the human psyche.

In the project nature is seen as a medium for communication and a source of healing within the therapeutic work. Nature is regarded as an ideal medium for therapeutic work largely due to the demographic of the client group with whom the Medical Foundation for the Care of Victims of Torture work. The client group is made up of those seeking refuge from their country of origin due to persecution for either political or social activities, having been subject to forms of imprisonment and torture resulting in psychological trauma. English is not the first language of the majority of the client group, and psychotherapy as it is predominantly practised in Europe, i.e. in a room, using language and psychological constructs to effect change, was anathema to the majority of participants. In this context the outdoors felt safe and the fact that language was not the primary medium for the therapeutic work was an important aspect in engaging people in the therapy in a non-threatening and supportive way. In this sense a room space is not always conducive to therapy for particular client groups.

In adopting a definition for the work that is defined as psychotherapy in a garden context, the approach is related to horticultural therapy but is predominantly focused not on gardening as a therapeutic occupation, but as a medium through which trauma can be understood and worked through. In working in a garden context, clients were asked to create things from the past which would help them come to terms with aspects of the trauma they had experienced. Trauma is re-encountered in the safe space of the garden, and the role of the psychotherapist in this process is to reflect experiences back to the client via contact with nature. Therapeutic work is carried out in a garden context and an allotment space, both containing rich material to work with.

Examples of this process consist of the use of nature as a metaphor for the human condition. In this sense the natural space is used 'projectively' in that the inner world is reflected back and encountered in metaphors that directly relate to client experience and can be worked with at a safe distance. For example, the relationship with plants and what they signify, particularly in relation to the client's country of origin, is used in the psychotherapeutic process to explore what has been lost from the clients' lives. The client's idealisations about the past and fears for the future are explored through the metaphor of growth and how things may develop differently in their new country.

The physical and aesthetic aspects of nature are important, in that smell, touch, sensate connection to the elements such as sun and rain, alongside the physical work of gardening, are all seen as part of a broad milieu of therapy. Linden and

Grut (2002) give examples of this where the physical work of weeding an allotment overrun with couch grass became for one client a process akin to pulling out the weeds he felt had grown in his mind and the rage he struggled to contain arising from his past traumatic experience. In methodically and patiently weeding his plot, the client engages with his rage and trauma and learns patience as part of this process. At the same time the client is weeding and repairing the damage he has done to his relationships, which is explored with the psychotherapist who works alongside the clients and engages in conversation as part of the practical and therapeutic work. By working in this way we can see how therapeutic work in nature has the potential to become more multifaceted with different forms of relationship coming into play between inner and outer reality. The therapist is not in one 'role' exclusively, but may be gardening alongside clients, whilst at the same time exploring feelings and thoughts in conversations which move between the therapeutic and the social. The psychotherapist loses the physical containment of the room space, therefore more emphasis is placed on psychological boundaries that are essential to good psychotherapeutic work, and the maturity of the therapist in understanding and negotiating different relationships and spaces. Linden and Grut (2002) describe how the therapist may be having tea and biscuits with clients and engaging in 'chit-chat' around therapeutic sessions. The therapeutic session may not be so clearly demarcated and may not last for the exact fifty-minute hour common to counselling and psychotherapy practice.

Some of these themes will be picked up in more depth later in the book when we explore the different facets of therapeutic process in relation to working outdoors and how this impacts upon the relationship with the therapist and what role nature plays in this. I will also look at the issue of holding a therapeutic frame in an outdoor context and some of the challenges and opportunities of this.

Nature therapy

Another attempt to bring therapeutic models to bear in relation to nature has been Ronen Berger's 'Nature Therapy' (Berger 2006). Nature therapy is a pluralistic approach to therapy, drawing upon a broad range of models such as art and drama therapy, gestalt and shamanism to articulate the model. In Berger's model, nature is seen as a live and dynamic partner in the therapeutic work, a third party in the process of therapy in the outdoors: nature as a co-therapist (Berger 2006: 268). Nature has a central role to play in instigating and mediating the therapeutic process, and is the therapeutic setting for the work, and therefore holds a central role in the relational dynamic of therapy (Berger and McLeod 2006). In contrasting this to a room environment, a space usually owned and controlled by the therapist for the purpose of therapy, nature therapy represents a more democratic space for the therapeutic work to unfold and therefore has an impact on the therapist–client relationship. Berger's research highlights how nature promotes a more democratic relationship in therapy, including the therapeutic alliance, hierarchy, authority and the therapeutic contract (Berger 2007).

Berger (2007) gives a clinical example of allowing a client to take ownership of the physical location of the therapy in order to 'build a home in nature', allowing the client autonomy in the process of how and in what ways he might build his home. The client constructs a therapeutic space that is very personal, using natural materials they find in the here and now. This is then explored in relation to the client's current issues. By developing a three-way relationship between client–therapist–nature, specific relational standpoints can be taken up by the therapist in relation to the work. The therapist may take a central role, as in traditional psychotherapeutic approaches, relating to nature as a backdrop or tool for the work. Equally they may take a role in the background of the therapeutic process which allows the client to work more directly with nature; as such the therapist acts as human witness, mediator and container for the work (Berger 2007: 6).

In linking the nature therapy to art and drama therapy, the use of metaphor and symbolism is central to the therapeutic process. Similarly to the natural growth project, both metaphor and nature's processes, e.g. a rain storm, provide rich material for analogies with life's challenges and existential dilemmas (Berger 2007: 7). Berger also positions nature as a sacred space for the therapy, and in this we can see links to shamanism and ritual which are central to his approach. This allows for the creation of a qualitatively different space than the mundane space of the client's life. This introduction of sacred and ritualised space allows for the client to explore facets of themselves not available in other areas of their life (Berger 2006; Berger and McLeod 2006).

Nature therapy outlines some important aspects of how, by incorporating nature into therapeutic practice, the 'space' of traditional therapy is changed. The relationship between therapist and client shifts in its power locus and becomes more democratic. Berger outlines some important aspects of nature's role in the therapeutic process and the dynamic relationship between therapist–client–nature, suggesting aspects of the therapist's stance within this which becomes more multifaceted. Some of the limitations of the approach are that Berger fails to articulate a meaningful discussion of practice issues, such as how to hold a secure therapeutic frame for nature therapy, and how to hold a therapeutic frame in a natural context.

Nature-guided therapy

In his approach, 'Nature-Guided Therapy' (Burns 1998), George Burns draws on the work of Milton Erickson foregrounding a more holistic idea of health at both a psychological and physical level, prioritising contact with the natural world to facilitate quick and effective changes. Erickson's approach pioneered behaviourally oriented approaches to psychotherapy alongside other forms of intervention such as brief therapy and solution-focused strategies. Erickson would often assign his clients tasks which involved interaction with nature (which has links with indigenous and traditional forms of healing; see Coggins 1990). These tasks involved the facilitation of the client's sensual awareness through contact with the natural world. For example, someone suffering from mild agoraphobia was told to focus on a 'flash of colour' when outside. She reported seeing a redheaded woodpecker fly past an evergreen tree and this facilitated looking for further flashes of colour and the lessening of her agoraphobia (Rosen 1982, cited in Burns 1998: 15).

Burns says our senses provide us with contact with the natural world, and it is via this sensate experience that emotional experience can be triggered. He sees the sensory experience not purely as a form of knowing, but as a way of experiencing the therapeutic effects of nature via the senses. Burns sees the importance of multimodal sensual experiences as part of the therapy process: the stimuli that are offered by natural environments are very different from those of indoor man-made rooms. He sees sensual awareness in this multimodal form as part of a process of being with nature, experiencing a holistic biological and emotional fit. The approach is focused on brief behavioural strategies which Burns says are solution-oriented, client-focused and pragmatic, enhancing motivation and focused on wellness, encouraging choice and empowerment (Burns 1998: 22).

Burns sees nature as providing two central processes that can be utilised for therapy. The first of these is through the stimulation that nature provides via its ever-changing myriad forms; for example no two sunsets are ever the same. In watching a sunset we discover a range of emotional responses which can be brought back and worked with in the therapy. Alongside this, the engagement of our senses via nature is of fundamental value therapeutically and nature can provide a range of pleasurable sensations. Burns (drawing from Erickson's example) directs clients in forms of contact with nature, administering a therapist-initiated sensual awareness directive. An example is given of one depressed client struggling with relationships, who is directed that when her alarm goes off she is to go down to the river bank, watch a sunrise and focus on visual stimuli. She reports back feeling better having watched several sunrises. Burns says these sensual contact directives move clients from an inner-directed symptom focus to more pleasurable techniques that can facilitate vital life-nourishing energies, assisting towards peak experiences and promoting a sense of health (1998: 73).

In positioning the sensual as an important part of therapeutic engagement with the natural world alongside psychological engagement, Burns highlights some arguments that are around, particularly in the ecopsychology literature, that point towards modernity's emotionally deadening effect on the psyche and the senses. This 'deadening' effect may be at the root of some mental health problems (Kidner 2007). Burns's understanding of nature-guided therapy takes psychotherapy into a more multidimensional process of sensate connection to the natural world. By positioning this as a central part in the therapy process Burns contributes to an enhanced understanding of a multidimensional therapeutic process in nature. Burns offers a way forward in expanding notions of how counselling and psychotherapy might engage with the therapeutic benefits of living natural processes on an aesthetic and sensory level, and in this way foregrounding psychotherapeutic processes in nature which are more multifaceted and holistic.

Adventure and wilderness therapy

Adventure therapy focuses on the challenge of contact with the outdoors and is normally carried out in association with some form of activity such as canoeing, rock climbing, high ropes work or some other form of adventurous activity which becomes the medium for therapeutic work (Richards and Peel 2005). Traditional forms of adventure therapy have tended to work with at-risk youth and more treatment-resistant groups. Ringer (2008) sees a difference in the sort of client groups most adventure and wilderness treatment programmes cater for, those with antisocial behaviour problems, rather than clients traditionally seen for group-based psychotherapy.

Outdoor therapies such as adventure and wilderness therapy are predominantly carried out with young people, and one of the main therapeutic aims is to improve the 'self concept' of the person participating. In this sense the predominant focus is on psychological issues and the approach draws heavily upon concepts from psychology such as improving self-efficacy (Schoel et al. 1988). The focus on the psychological interiority of the person participating, independent of particular contexts, shares common factors with wilderness therapy (Berman and Berman 1994; Moore and Russell 2002), and outdoor behavioural healthcare (Russell and Hendee 2000), an approach helping adolescents overcome emotional, adjustment, addiction and other psychological problems. Ringer (2008) errs on the side of flexibility, ambiguity and generalisation in defining adventure therapy, seeing it as defying definition; rather its various forms can be found in adventure therapy programmes. He sees a number of key elements which programmes need to contain which then means they coalesce around the label 'adventure therapy'. These include the setting for the work as either outdoor or wilderness, adventure activities, spiritual/cultural elements, psychotherapeutic approaches and group and relationship dynamics. This broad definition has led to the development of a burgeoning field, but also to a lot of confusion about what constitutes 'therapy' in these programmes and what the role of the natural world might be. Indeed 'wilderness therapy' is often considered to be a distinct form of adventure therapy, where at-risk youth are placed in remote areas and physically challenged in terms of self-care and group process as a way of re-socialising them back into urban environments (Ringer 2008; Davis-Berman and Berman 2009). The similarity between these approaches has led to much confusion between terms, purpose and activity, leading to a lack of clarity as to the focus of programmes as therapeutic, educational or developmental. For the purpose of my research, how the therapists foreground the inner world of the participants and how this relates to the outer world is an important aspect of therapeutic work that needs to be taken into account when exploring therapeutic change and how counselling and psychotherapy might work in the outdoors. However, the idea of nature as a therapeutic space is under-theorised and accounted for in these programmes. Nature is seen as a place to be utilised, not as another meaningful relationship central to the therapeutic process. This has led some authors to criticise approaches such as adventure therapy as failing to account for the therapeutic dimensions of nature contact in and of itself, arguing that because of the dominant paradigm of psychology, the healing effects of nature are under-recognised and incorporated into theories (Beringer 1999).

Greenway (1995) has pointed out what he sees as the considerable confusion in the use of wilderness for therapy and the difficulty the field has in articulating what might be 'the wilderness effect'. Indeed, Greenway asks, if in most forms of wilderness and adventure therapy interior psychological change (independent of the natural context) is the goal, why go out into natural areas in the first place if psychological change could possibly be best served in urban environments. Greenway (2009) argues that the central 'disease' of our late modern culture is the problem of the human–nature relationship and it is this that should be the central focus of any psychotherapy. Philosophically, the field of adventure and wilderness therapy seems to be caught in a split between mind and nature and where both might sit within dominant cultural and knowledge frameworks. It is my contention that this split reflects problems in the theoretical and knowledge bases underpinning adventure and wilderness therapy. The literature also fails to meaningfully discuss any issues of the 'frame' or boundaries which I see as central to counselling and psychotherapy practice (see later section for fuller elaboration), assuming these are an unproblematic part of the therapeutic work.

Horticultural therapy

Drawing upon research in environmental psychology that positions nature as important for psychological restoration and stress reduction (Kaplan and Kaplan 1989; Ulrich 2000), horticultural therapy places contact with plants and nature as beneficial to emotional and psychological health, reducing the stress of urban living (Ulrich and Parsons 1990).

A definition of horticultural therapy and therapeutic horticulture is given by Growth Point:

> Horticultural therapy is the use of plants by a trained professional as a medium through which certain clinically defined goals may be met. Therapeutic horticulture is the process by which individuals may develop well-being using plants and horticulture. This is achieved by active or passive involvement.
>
> (Growth Point 1999: 4)

As anecdotal evidence points out and research identifies (Ulrich and Parsons 1990), passive experiencing of plants enhances well-being and health, reducing stress and negative thoughts. It may be that this passive backdrop to therapy conducted in outdoor natural spaces provides a beneficial context for therapy to be conducted.

A more active engagement with plants through horticultural activities shares a lot of common features with the goals of occupational therapy (Palsdottir et al. 2013). These activities both have clearly defined clinical goals which are located within the context of a wider social care milieu. These goals might include the development of motor skills through physical activity, the development of cognitive skills through the process of comprehension, judgement and memory, as well as groups and social interaction as part of an overall treatment plan (Hewson 1994). The natural growth project represents a clear example of where the theories and practice of psychotherapy are applied to horticulture and activities both within a garden and within an allotment context.

Scandinavian healing and rehabilitation gardens

In Sweden in the 1990s a growing number of the population were succumbing to the effects of work-related stress and what was termed 'burn out disease' due to changes in the labour market. Interestingly Grahn et al. (2007) refer to 'burn out disease' as a form of 'vital exhaustion', an existential life crisis where people have lost touch with themselves and their abilities to cope. Specially designed gardens were developed with structured and unstructured elements, staffed by multi-disciplinary teams comprising a gardener, occupational therapist and psycho-therapist, alongside a psychiatrist, in order to aid people in their recovery from stress-related disorders (Sahlin et al. 2012). The model originated from a specially designed health garden on the campus of the Swedish University of Agricultural Sciences in Alnarp, Sweden. The two-hectare garden was designed according to theories on restorative and supportive environments with a focus on holism as an intervention. The garden was divided into different areas with various charac-teristics and structures, in order to meet the emerging needs and moods of participants during their rehabilitation. As part of the programme participants could use the garden freely according to their own needs and desires to support their rehabilitation process, which could be in the form of active or more passive experiences of nature (Grahn et al. 2010).

Further work and research has developed in Denmark at the Danish Centre for Forest, Landscape and Planning at the University of Copenhagen in a research project called 'The Healing Forest Garden Nacadia', the aims of which were to develop and practise 'nature-based therapy' in a specially designed healing garden and to conduct longitudinal effect studies (Corazon et al. 2010). Corazon et al. (2012) propose a model of nature-based therapy which incorporates aspects of mindfulness and acceptance and commitment therapy (ACT) within a permaculture framework, bringing together activities of both psychotherapy and gardening. Nature-based metaphors are implemented as a therapeutic tool in relation to activities and experiences. For example, issues of embodiment and concepts of self in relationships, as well as being in the present moment, are all incorporated into garden activities and processes. The Scandinavian healing gardens represent a practice-based intervention supported by ongoing research which takes our understanding of nature-based therapies forward.

Ecotherapy and ecopsychology

In some senses ecotherapy and ecopsychology are central to understanding psychotherapy in nature as they speak of the idea of a reciprocal relationship with nature that is central to mental health. Ecopsychology's core hypothesis is that the movement away from the natural world due to the conditions of industrialisation is at the root of human psychological distress, and this distanciation is at the heart of the rampant ecological destruction inflicted by man upon the natural world. Roszak (1992) argues that a psychological theory that does not address itself to this irrationality on such a grand scale is deeply flawed. Ecotherapy draws, particularly in the United States, on ideas from ecopsychology that propose therapeutic practices which seek to heal this split (Buzzell and Chalquist 2009).

Ecopsychology's fundamental contribution to the underpinning theory of counselling and psychotherapy in the outdoors is to place the split between psyche and the natural world as central to human well-being and subsequent distress. How the concept of the 'split' between mind and nature is theorised and understood is by no means unproblematic, especially in the way it presents nature and the natural, and also the complex relationship of where ecology sits in relation to psychology.

Clinebell first coined the term ecotherapy in his book, *Ecotherapy: Healing Ourselves, Healing the Earth* (Clinebell 1996). Clinebell posits a form of 'ecological spirituality' whereby our holistic relationship with nature encompasses both nature's ability to nurture us, through our contact with natural places and spaces, and our ability to reciprocate this healing connection through our ability to nurture nature. In this sense ecotherapy has always shared a close relationship with ecopsychology (Roszak et al. 1995), placing human–nature relationships within a reciprocal healing (and disconnected and destructive) relationship with nature. Clinebell (1996: xxi) makes a distinction, preferring to use the term ecotherapy over ecopsychology, stating that ecopsychology is about the psyche and the 'greening of psychology', whereas ecotherapy focuses on the total mind-body-spirit-relationship organism. Recent developments, particularly in America, have placed ecotherapy in the role of 'practising clinician', viewing ecotherapy as 'applied' or clinical ecopsychology, just as psychotherapy can be described as applied or clinical psychology (Jordan 2009b). Ecotherapy is positioned as healing the human–nature relationship, and includes a range of therapeutic and reconnective practices such as horticultural therapy, 'green' exercise, animal-assisted therapy, wilderness therapy, natural lifestyle therapy, eco-dreamwork, community ecotherapy, dealing with eco-anxiety and eco-grief, and much more (Buzzell and Chalquist 2009). More recently the charity MIND published an evaluation report on ecotherapy (MIND 2013), which found that people's mental health significantly improved after activities in nature. The MIND report highlighted its own definition of ecotherapy, referring to horticultural development programmes supervised by a therapist or a simple walk in the park; this encompasses differing versions of what ecotherapy might or could be.

The book *Ecotherapy: Healing with Nature in Mind* (Buzzell and Chalquist 2009) forms a challenge to traditional ideas of psychotherapy as conducted within an indoor environment abstracted from the context of nature and the outside world. 'Ecotherapy' is used as an umbrella term for nature-based methods of physical and psychological healing. Buzzell and Chalquist (2009) argue that it represents a new form of psychotherapy which acknowledges the vital role of nature and addresses the human–nature relationship. Ecotherapy gives a client permission to talk about a wider matrix of relationships that are important in their life, for example with animals or plants. Traditional therapy approaches have not tended to see these relationships with the more-than-human world (i.e. with nature and other sentient beings such as animals) as an important part of how the client's story and healing intertwine (Hegarty 2010).

Hasbach (2012) has written about some of the confusions surrounding the term ecotherapy. In the UK the term has come to be linked with green exercise and horticultural activities (MIND 2007) not necessarily anything to do with psychotherapy. However, Hasbach argues against the notion that just by going out into nature for a walk we are engaging in ecotherapy. She defines ecotherapy as a new modality of therapy that enlarges the traditional scope of treatment to include the human–nature relationship (2012: 116).

In this manner ecotherapy fails to fully answer fundamental questions I have about the human-to-human dimensions of distress, how these interweave with human and nature relationships and the subsequent distress caused by these relationships. The idea that urbanised, industrial society and its dominance and distance from the natural world are at the heart of our distress does not fully and meaningfully account for the developmental and relational processes that I experience in my psychotherapy practice. It is the human-to-human problems that seem to cause many aspects of most clients' difficulties. It is also interesting to note that suicide rates amongst farmers and others who live rurally are not significantly lower than those in urban areas, and in fact may be higher (Judd et al. 2006). Thus it can be argued that the relationship between internal and external worlds, between geographical location and mental health, is more complex than perhaps ecotherapy might have us believe. This leaves me with some questions: how might ideas from contemporary psychotherapy theory and practice interweave with ideas from the emerging fields of ecopsychology and ecotherapy? How might some of the practicalities of taking people into natural environments, which are utilised in forms of adventure and wilderness therapy, translate into psychotherapy practices which hold the fifty-minute session in a room as sacrosanct? Overall, how might we articulate the therapeutic effects of the natural world and our relationships with it?

Arts therapies: symbols, aesthetics and embodied experience

Arts therapies represent a movement in therapy away from a predominantly verbal dialogue with two people sitting in chairs. Arts therapies see the medium of the art form and expression of creativity as central to the therapeutic and healing effect of therapy. The medium of expression and its symbolic content are of central importance to the therapeutic process. Some forms of art therapy have gravitated towards the idea of art as a bridge towards verbal therapy, with others fore-grounding the healing power of the art work itself, the aesthetics of experience and perception. The danger is that these two positions become polarised between the sensibilities of the artist and the psychological focus of the psychotherapist (Robbins 1994). Aesthetics is understood as the philosophical study of beauty in the form of art, taste, experience and its psychological affects. Robbins (1994) sees the 'beautiful' as what comes alive, where the inanimate becomes animate. So for Robbins what becomes beautiful in art therapy is in the art work itself or in the transitional space between the client and the therapist.

The land art movement (Tiberghien 1995; Kastner 1998) explores the aesthetic and reconnective power of art as it is embedded in the landscape. This kind of art literally makes art out of the raw materials of the natural space where it takes place and can be seen in the works of artists such as Andy Goldsworthy (2004). Goldsworthy's aesthetic could be described as a deep connection and understanding of natural space and place and how art can interweave with nature to represent a narrative of a living space. Art again here represents a pictorial narrative beyond just words and is an attempt to develop a language of human–nature relationships embodied in visual forms.

The arts therapies have foregrounded the importance of symbolic content through the medium of art, in the form of creativity, movement, dance, drama and music therapy, and its representation as a vehicle and a process via which both conscious and unconscious material can be understood. In expressive arts therapy 'art' is understood as a broad and plural multiplicity, characterised by any art making and considered fundamental to human experience (Knill 1999; Waller 2005). Use of symbolism and metaphor can be seen in the work of Ronan Berger (2006). His approach, 'building a home in nature', draws heavily from ideas and practices in art and drama therapy, but also importantly introduces nature as a 'third' in the process, an additional presence to the client–therapist dyad (Berger and McLeod 2006).

This idea of the aesthetics of experience and its psychological and emotional affects becomes more important in therapy in outdoor natural spaces because another element is introduced into the therapeutic process: the natural environment. In this sense we can see similarities with the arts therapies and how symbol, experience and process in the form of creativity become important either as a medium to access interior psychological material or on an aesthetic experiential level that is therapeutic in and of itself. The senses and sensory contact become more prominent in outdoor natural spaces in terms of the feel of air, warmth, touch, hearing and smell.

Frizell (2008) argues that creative arts therapies are, by their very nature, concerned with the expression of an inner world which transcends words. Frizell proposes that dance movement therapy leads us into the world of sensory perception, into a physical and spiritual expression through which our emotions flow; it is through embodied connection that we find connection as dynamic organisms to the diversity of a living world. This sense of an embodied experience beyond words which connects to wider living dynamic systems also seems an important part of understanding therapeutic process and how it might link to a wider living matrix in the practice of counselling and psychotherapy in nature. The importance of the aesthetic and symbolic in arts-based psychotherapy foregrounds the importance of the relational space of the therapy and the effect this has on participants.

Concluding comments

In this chapter I have explored the field of nature-based therapies. There are particular approaches to working therapeutically outdoors which provide a lot of useful insight, theoretical and case discussion, and can inform ways of working outdoors, not least of which is the growing field of ecotherapy. There are some specific areas in the literature that are not covered fully or in enough depth to support a therapist who, trained to work indoors, wants to understand the unique aspects of holding a therapeutic frame in an outdoor context and certain aspects of how the therapeutic relationship and process are affected by the move outside. These will be covered in the following chapters.

References

Berger, R. (2006) Beyond words: nature-therapy in action. *Journal of Critical Psychology, Counseling and Psychotherapy* 6(4), 195–199.

Berger, R. (2007) Nature therapy: developing a framework for practice. Unpublished PhD, School of Health and Social Sciences. University of Abertay, Dundee.

Berger, R. and McLeod, J. (2006) Incorporating nature into therapy: a framework for practice. *Journal of Systemic Therapies* 25(2), 80–94.

Beringer, A. (1999) On adventure therapy and earth healing: toward a sacred cosmology. *Australian Journal of Outdoor Education* 4(1), 33–39.

Berman, J. and Berman, D. (1994) *Wilderness Therapy: Foundations Theory and Research.* Iowa: Kendall Hunt.

Bridges, N. A. (1999) Psychodynamic perspective on therapeutic boundaries: creative clinical possibilities. *Journal of Psychotherapy Research and Practice* 8(4), 292–300.

Burns, G. (1998) *Nature Guided Therapy: Brief Integrative Strategies for Health and Well-Being.* London: Taylor & Francis.

Buzzell, L. and Chalquist, C. (2009) *Ecotherapy: Healing with Nature in Mind.* San Francisco: Sierra Club.

Clinebell, H. (1996) *Ecotherapy: Healing Ourselves, Healing the Earth: A Guide to Ecologically Grounded Personality Theory, Spirituality, Therapy, and Education.* London: Fortress.

Coggins, K. (1990) *Alternative Pathways to Healing.* Florida: Health Communications, Inc.

Corazon, S. S., Stigsdotter, U. K., Nielsen, A. G. and Nilsson, K. (2010) Developing the nature based therapy concept for people with stress related illness at the Danish healing forest garden Nacadia. *Journal of Therapeutic Horticulture* 20, 35–50.

Corazon, S. S., Stigsdotter, U. K. and Rasmussen, S. M. (2012) Nature as therapist: integrating permaculture with mindfulness and acceptance based therapy in the healing forest garden Nacadia. *European Journal of Psychotherapy and Counselling* 14(4), 335–347.

Davies-Berman, J. and Berman, D. (2009) *The Promise of Wilderness Therapy.* Association of Experiential Education.

Frizell, C. (2008) In search of the wider self. *E-Motion* 1, 1281–1287.

Gass, M., Lee-Gillis, H. L. and Russell, K. C. (2012) *Adventure Therapy: Theory, Research and Practice.* London: Routledge.

Goldsworthy, A. (2004) *Passage.* London: Thames & Hudson.

Grahn, P., Bengtsson, I. L., Welen-Andersson, L., Lindofrs, L., Tauchnitz, F. and Tenngart, C. (2007) Alnarp rehabilitation garden: possible health effects from the design, from the activities and from the therapeutic team. Open Space Conference Proceedings. www.openspace.eca.ac.uk/conference/proceedings/PDF/Hartig.pdf.

Grahn, P., Tenngart Ivarsson, C., Stigsdotter, U. and Bengtsson, I.-L. (2010) Using affordances as a health promoting tool in a therapeutic garden. In C. Ward Thompson, P. Aspinall and S. Bell (eds) *Innovative Approaches to Researching Landscape and Health.* Open Space: People Space 2. New York: Routledge, pp. 116–154.

Greenway, R. (1995) The wilderness effect and ecopsychology. In T. Roszak, M. Gomes and A. Kanner (eds) *Ecopsychology: Restoring the Earth, Healing the Mind.* London: Sierra Club.

Greenway, R. (2009) The wilderness experience as therapy: we've been here before. In L. Buzzell and C. Chalquist (eds) *Ecotherapy – Healing with Nature in Mind.* San Francisco: Sierra Club.

Growth Point (1999) Your future starts here: practitioners determine the way ahead. *Growth Point* 79, 4–5.

Hasbach, P. (2012) Ecotherapy. In P. Kahn and P. Hasbach (eds) *Ecopsychology: Science, Totems and the Technological Species.* London: MIT Press.

Hegarty, J. (2010) Out of the consulting room and into the woods? Experiences of nature-connectedness and self-healing. *European Journal of Ecopsychology* 1, 64–84.

Hewson, M. (1994) *Horticulture as Therapy.* Ontario: Homewood Health Centre.

Jordan, M. (2009a) Nature and self: an ambivalent attachment? *Ecopsychology* 1(1), 26–31.

Jordan, M. (2009b) Back to nature. *Therapy Today* 20(3), 26–28.

Jordan, M. (2009c) The living mountain: attachment to landscape and its importance in regulating emotions. *Journal of Holistic Healthcare* 6(3), 14–17.

Jordan, M. and Marshall, H. (2010) Taking therapy outside: deconstructing or reconstructing the therapeutic frame? *European Journal of Psychotherapy and Counselling* 12(4), 345–359.

Judd, F., Cooper, A., Fraser, C. and Davis, J. (2006) Rural suicide – people or place effects? *Australian and New Zealand Journal of Psychiatry* 40(3), 208–216.

Kaplan, S. and Kaplan, R. (1989) *The Experience of Nature.* Cambridge: Cambridge University Press.

Kastner, J. (1998) *Land and Environmental Art (Themes and Movement).* London: Phaidon Inc.

Kidner, D. W. (2007) Depression and the natural world: towards a critical ecology of psychological distress. *International Journal of Critical Psychology* 19(Spring), 123–143.

Knill, P. J. (1999) Soul nourishment, or the intermodal language of imagination. In S. K. Levine and E. G. Levine (eds) *Foundations of Expressive Arts Therapy: Theoretical and Clinical Perspectives.* London: Jessica Kingsley.

Linden, S. and Grut, J. (2002) *The Healing Fields: Working with Psychotherapy and Nature to Rebuild Shattered Lives.* London: Frances Lincoln.

MIND (2007) *Ecotherapy: The Green Agenda for Mental Health.* London: MIND.

MIND (2013) *Feel Better Outside, Feel Better Inside: Ecotherapy for Mental Wellbeing, Resilience and Recovery.* London: MIND.

Mitchell, S. (1988) *Relational Concepts within Psychoanalysis: An Integration.* Cambridge, MA: Harvard University Press.

Moore, T. and Russell, K. (2002) *Studies of the Use of Wilderness for Personal Growth, Therapy, Education, and Leadership Development: An Annotation and Evaluation.* University of Idaho Wilderness Research Centre College of Natural Resources, University of Idaho, USA.

Palsdottir, A. M., Grahn, P. and Persson, D. (2013) Changes in experienced value of everyday occupations after nature-based vocational rehabilitation. *Scandinavian Journal of Occupational Therapy.* Early Online, 1–11.

Richards, K. and Peel, J. (2005) Outdoor cure. *Therapy Today* 16(10), 3–8.

Ringer, M. (2008) A subjective description of adventure therapy. *Journal of Outdoor Activities* 1(1), 8–15.

Robbins, A. (1994) The play of psychotherapeutic artistry and psychoaesthetics. In A. Robbins (ed.) *A Multimodal Approach to Creative Arts Therapy.* London: Jessica Kingsley.

Rosen, S. (1982) *My Voice Will Go with You: The Teaching Tales of Milton H. Erickson, MD.* New York: Norton.

Roszak, T. (1992) *The Voice of the Earth.* London: Simon & Schuster.

Roszak, T., Gomes, M. and Kanner, A. (1995) *Ecopsychology: Restoring the Earth, Healing the Mind.* London: Sierra Club.

Russell, K. and Hendee, J. (2000). *Defining and Cataloguing the Outdoor Behavioural Healthcare Industry: A National Survey of Programs.* University of Idaho Wilderness Research Centre College of Natural Resources, University of Idaho, USA.

Sahlin, E., Matuszczyk, J. F., Ahlborg, Jr. G. and Grahn, P. (2012) How do participants in nature-based therapy experience and evaluate their rehabilitation? *Journal of Therapeutic Horticulture* 22(1), 9–22.

Santostefano, S. (2004) *Child Therapy in the Great Outdoors: A Relational View.* London: Hillside Press.

Schoel, J., Prouty, D. and Radcliffe, P. (1988) *Islands of Healing: A Guide to Adventure Based Counseling.* London: Kendall/Hunt.

Tiberghien, G. A. (1995) *Land Art.* New York: Princeton Architectural Press.

Ulrich, R. (2000) Effects of gardens on health outcomes: theory and research. In C. Marcus and M. Barnes (eds) *Healing Gardens: Therapeutic Benefits and Design Recommendations.* Chichester: Wiley.

Ulrich, R. and Parsons, R. (1990) Influences of passive experiences with plants on individual well-being and health. In D. Relf (ed.) *The Role of Horticulture in Human Well-Being and Social Development: A National Symposium.* Portland, OR: Timber Press.

Waller, D. (2005) *Arts, Therapies, Communication: Different Approaches to a Unique Discipline*, vol. III (with Kossalapow, L. and Scoble, S.). Munster: Lit Verlag.

Chapter 3

The therapeutic relationship and nature-based therapy

I want to start this chapter by positioning therapy outdoors within a broader understanding of counselling and psychotherapy, the therapeutic relationship and how change processes happen within the therapeutic encounter. I will also look at attachment to nature and the role nature might play in the therapeutic relationship, particularly the role it may play as a transitional object. One of the weaknesses of the literature on nature-based therapies is the absence of a strong and coherent link to mainstream counselling and psychotherapy approaches. The relational perspective draws upon a variety of ideas that are not related purely to one particular school in counselling and psychotherapy. Central tenets of the approach are the idea that psychological phenomena develop within a broad field of relationships, both from the past and in the present, and that experience within the therapeutic encounter is continually and mutually shaped by both participants (Bridges 1999). The approach draws upon ideas from self-psychology, psychodynamic developmental psychology, feminist psychology, and intersubjectivity theory.

The relational paradigm in counselling and psychotherapy

Relational psychotherapy states that well-being depends on having satisfying mutual relationships with others; the concept of a reciprocal mutual relationship is important for psychotherapy. The origin of emotional distress is often rooted in patterns of relational experience, past and present, which have the power to demean and deaden the self. The relational therapist tries to experience and understand the client's unique self-experience in its social/relational context and to respond with empathy and genuine presence. Together, client and therapist create a new in-depth relationship which is supportive, strengthening, and enlivening for the client; Mitchell (1988) sees the end result as the healing of disordered subjectivity. Within this secure relationship, the client can safely re-experience, and then find freedom from, the powerful effects of destructive relationships both past and present.

In relational psychotherapy the meanings given to experience, rather than any underpinning biological drives, become important in understanding the distress that the client is experiencing. The therapeutic process involves both client and therapist negotiating, interacting and co-constructing old and new experiences in relationship. The approach draws upon ideas from constructivism, arguing that the mind (and its intrapsychic contents) does not exist in isolation, but is embedded in an intersubjective field which creates meaning (Stolorow and Atwood 1992). The approach emphasises mutual participation, influencing and regulation between therapist and client, with at least one author emphasising the embodiment of this process as being central to therapeutic change (Santostefano 2004).

Transference and counter transference

My understanding of the therapeutic relationship comes from the ideas of writers such as Kohut (1971), Winnicott (1958), Bowlby (1969) and Stolorow and Atwood (1992), all of whom see the relationship between caregiver and infant as central to healthy emotional development. From this view development of the 'self' forms in relationship to others in the infant's world and disruptions that occur in this relationship lead to problems in the infant's sense of self (Stern 1985). Key to helping bring change in these distortions of self is the relationship that can be formed with the therapist.

There are some central components of the therapeutic relationship that manifest as a process of the therapeutic encounter. Transference was initially identified by Freud (1912) as a pattern of relating to both the therapist and others in the client's life which originates from early experience with caregivers, predominantly the child's parents. Transference issues manifest in the process of therapy in terms of how the client feels towards the therapist, their needs and conflicts. Often these issues can manifest around the frame of therapy in terms of timing of sessions, whether the client arrives late and finds it difficult to end the therapy, how the client feels about the therapist's breaks and holidays. What also emerged, as the later school of object relations developed and moved away from Freudian drive theory, was the process of counter transference. This was understood as the therapist's emotional reaction to the client's transference issues (Heimann 1950). The emotions the therapist experiences during the therapy sessions become central to understanding the emotional material of the client that is sometimes held out of awareness or is unconscious. In this sense the intersubjective space between therapist and client contains the affective material that is central to understanding and conducting counselling and psychotherapy. Gill (1982) has emphasised the importance of re-experiencing in the therapeutic process, believing that as the client's problems were caused experientially they will be transformed experientially, and cannot be reasoned away intellectually. Therefore the therapy process becomes one where the client can feel safe and held enough to re-experience some of the initial emotional difficulties that brought them to therapy in the first place.

I see personal therapy, supervision and ongoing reflexive emotional engagement as central to my practice and understanding of counselling and psychotherapy. Personal therapy, which I had for the four years of my psychotherapy training, was central to understanding my own development and emotional world; also, to experience 'being a client' allowed me to understand the experience of therapy from both perspectives.

Therapeutic process and understanding how change occurs in psychotherapy

Contemporary research into how and why psychotherapy works has either focused on outcomes in terms of symptom reduction and increased well-being in order to ascertain the effectiveness of particular forms of therapy, or instead has tended to focus on the 'process' of psychotherapy, attempting to identify what happens and is of significance for both therapist and client in the therapeutic encounter. What the research tells us is that in terms of outcomes, no one therapeutic approach is clearly the winner in terms of established effectiveness. Cognitive behavioural therapy may do well in terms of its measured efficacy for particular clinical populations under specific controlled conditions, but may not be as effective in maintaining change over an extended period of time post-therapy. It is clear that more research needs to be undertaken in both the emerging field of green care and in particular nature-based therapy, in terms of outcomes, to support the growing interest in these forms of intervention. However my particular focus is understanding how some forms of therapeutic process work in a natural setting and how some of these concepts might usefully contribute towards an enhanced understanding of change processes when counselling and psychotherapy are conducted in natural spaces.

The Boston Change Process Study Group (2010) has written extensively about change processes in psychotherapy and what may be contributing factors in understanding how change works in psychotherapy. I have chosen this approach in particular as it links to a relational perspective within counselling and psychotherapy, draws upon psychoanalytic ideas in relation to transference and counter transference, sees the intersubjective encounter within therapy as an important factor, has a focus on implicit process that is beyond language-based interventions, and locates itself empirically within a growing body of infant research and neuroscientific evidence. Also, it links strongly with Daniel Stern's writings (indeed he is a member of the group) and the way connections can be made between some of the concepts discussed by the group and Stern's emphasis on the importance of forms of vitality in the therapeutic encounter that were outlined in Chapter 1.

The group sees change within the therapeutic encounter as an emergent dynamic and multifaceted process, with movement and flux as central. Change is co-created and occurs in the moment-to-moment interactions between the intersubjective worlds of both therapist and client. Local-level processes become important rather than making the client 'fit' a particular therapeutic theory or technique. These local-level processes, created in the unique encounter of therapist and client, can at times be sloppy, non-linear, non-causal and quite unpredictable. What is important in the therapeutic encounter is the co-creation of the surprising and useful events which happen from moment to moment or in particular 'moments of meeting', so rather than excavating pre-formed meanings there is a complex interaction between two minds in relation.

The group proposes 'implicit relational knowing' as an important concept, based on infant observation studies which position the pre-verbal infant as interacting with caregivers on the basis of a great deal of existent relational knowledge which is pre-verbal. Regulation of the infant through mother–infant interaction occurs from moment to moment through perceptual systems, with states such as hunger, sleep, arousal and forms of social contact, all of which need to be regulated through activities such as amplifying, elaborating, repairing and scaffolding, which bring the infant into a state of equilibrium. This regulation is also mutual, but necessarily asymmetrical with the caregiver doing a lot of the work, and occurs through a process of 'moving along' to an unspecified goal. This translates in therapy as the central process of affect attunement, through mutual regulation and the promotion of intersubjective understanding and self-awareness (BSPCG 2010).

'Now moments' in therapy are times when the therapy gets lit up subjectively and affectively, where both parties are pulled more fully into the present. These 'now moments' are usually distinct from the moment-to-moment process of therapy as it moves along. A 'now moment' that is seized therapeutically and mutually realised is a 'moment of meeting'; this is a highly specific event where each partner has contributed something unique and authentic of his or herself. The therapist must use a specific aspect of his or her individuality in this moment, not some theory or technique; it is something out of the usual or habitual way of operating in the therapy. These intimate intersubjective moments change the implicit relational knowing of the therapist–client relationship and are mutative events in the therapy (BSPCG 2010: 19). In understanding therapy as a constantly moving intersubjective process of moment-to-moment encounters, punctuated by unique and specific moments of meeting helping the therapy in moving along towards an evolving and changing goal, the group proposes that replacing past deficits is not the goal, but as reconceptualisation occurs in the implicit and explicit relational knowing of the client, a person can operate in an altered mental landscape.

Relational therapeutic process in nature

Nature is not static (as we explored in Chapter 1) and neither are human emotions or consciousness. Therefore we need to begin to understand how an emotional process might unfold when working therapeutically in nature. If we place nature within a dynamic relational matrix of nature–client–therapist we can then begin to see the therapeutic processes that come into play in relation to counselling and psychotherapy outdoors.

The Boston Change Process Study Group (2010) outlines some of the features they see as central to change processes within psychotherapy. The process of 'moving along' to a goal of understanding is central to the process of change: both therapist and client move along together in a process of unfolding understanding, which is creative and dynamic. When we place this in the context of an outdoor natural space, both therapist and client are located in a space that is dynamic and unfolding, possessing vital qualities that offer opportunities both for further understanding and for exploration in the therapeutic work.

In the course of 'moving along' in the therapeutic work with each other and within the natural setting, 'now moments' occur which are qualitatively different and unpredicted. As stated, BCPSG (2010) see these moments as 'hot' and containing 'moments of truth'; they stand out from the normal and habitual moments of therapy. When a now moment is seized and mutually recognised it can become a 'moment of meeting'. This requires both parties to bring uniqueness and authenticity, and something of themselves, to the therapeutic encounter. This happens in singular fashion, 'on the spot' as it were, and cannot be fashioned into some pre-existing therapeutic technique or manoeuvre. The intersubjective process between therapist and client is pushed into a zone that is more unstable, causing each party to have to do something 'new', and this causes a re-evaluation of the implicit relational knowing in both their subjectivities. The natural environment may offer opportunities to provoke these 'hot moments'; this is especially so because of the greater mutuality in the therapeutic process between therapist, client and nature. After the moment of meeting, an 'open space' occurs between therapist and client, where both disengage from their meeting and are able to be alone together in order to gather their thoughts and assimilate to find a new equilibrium. This is based on the work of Sander (1988) and infant–mother observation studies. I will give an example.

Case example

I was walking and talking with a client and she was sharing with me her concerns about the irregularity of her periods and how heavy and draining they were. She had presented herself to her doctors with a fear that she had cancer; after ruling out the possibility the doctor tried to reassure her that she didn't have cancer. In this sense we were moving along as usual in the therapy, both psychologically and physically; she quite often complained of illness and a fear that something was wrong with her. At this point in the session she managed to slip on the muddy path, falling down on one knee; as I helped her up, she stated with anger 'I hate my body'. I was struck by a realisation of how present this had been in the therapy but unspoken. We stopped at this point for her to gather herself and I shared with her how important it was for her to tell me this, how I felt that we had both 'known' this but that it had never been out in the open between us. It was a moment of meeting, a 'now moment' which felt qualitatively different from other moments in the therapy. In discussing this she opened up more and said how split she felt between her body and her mind; I shared how important I felt this realisation was for both of us to the therapy. It was a moment of meeting that allowed both of us to shift our intersubjective understanding of each other. We then sat for a moment in silence before we got up and started walking again.

The therapeutic relationship within an outdoor natural context

Conducting therapy within an outdoor natural space appears to have an effect on the therapeutic relationship between therapist and client. It has been pointed out by other writers in the field that nature has a democratising influence on the therapeutic relationship (Berger 2006). Nature can also act as an intermediary between the therapist and client. For example there may be some clients who feel the intensity of sitting in a room across from a therapist who is looking at them by maintaining a degree of eye contact too threatening. This may be particularly acute for those who have had more complex and difficult early experiences which have led to difficulties in attachment patterns and maintaining intimacy with another. Berger (2006) in his research into nature therapy discusses the idea of nature as a 'co-therapist' in the process of nature-based therapy. It is through the presence of the natural world that the therapeutic process is facilitated; nature in this sense acts as another presence which both guides and provokes the therapeutic work.

The power dynamic between therapist and client also seems to be affected. For certain clients, moving outside of a room space and walking with the therapist may help to break down a sense of professional distance, and this can also work both ways. In a negative sense it can make it much harder for the therapist to maintain a therapeutic focus for the work in the traditional sense of how they have been trained. However, for other clients it can facilitate a greater sense of relaxation and connection to the therapist which allows them to open up and feel safer in a shared space rather than in a room controlled by the therapist.

In terms of transference and counter transference this can be interesting. This affect on the transference points towards a process whereby taking therapy out of its traditional arena affects the power dynamics between client and therapist. If we think about the therapist's office as being a space largely controlled by either the therapist or the agency that the therapist is working within, we can see how it is possible for clients to feel disempowered in this environment and how it may even reinforce the powerlessness and victimhood of the client (Proctor 2010). The natural world may act as a democratising influence on the therapeutic process in that neither therapist nor client own or even control the space; it is 'shared' between both parties (Berger 2007). In this sense we can see why there may be more opportunities for mutuality in the therapeutic process, and this would link to contemporary developments within therapy. The relational school of thought posits a real relationship working alongside a transferential and counter-transferential process, allowing both client and therapist to experience each other's humanity (Bridges 1999; Mitchell 1988).

Case example

When asked how they were feeling about the therapeutic process outdoors a client recounted this explanation to the therapist: '... the experience of being in a natural and therefore to me, neutral space. When entering a therapist's space, generally a consultancy room, the environment of the room generally influences my preconceptions of the therapist, the relationship I will have with them and the support I will get. My experience of therapy was that my relationship with the environment – natural surroundings, and as much 'mine' as the therapist's – separated from my relationship with the therapist, immediately making me feel safer, on supportive ground; to the extent that the environment became the therapist and the "therapist" became a facilitator. The experience of feeling "I am in the therapist's territory", which I find sometimes unsettling, and the "patient/ professional" dynamic which can also be difficult, were both diminished' (Jordan and Marshall 2010: 349).

From a relational perspective the greater mutuality within the therapeutic relationship is part of the therapeutic process and represents a shift in therapeutic understanding of how the therapeutic relationship unfolds between therapist and client. In our article, Hayley Marshall and I wrote about this process and its effect on the therapeutic relationship. One of the challenges in working outdoors is how to hold the important, inherent, asymmetry of the therapeutic relationship whilst promoting mutuality in a natural environment that is more neutral; the latter often having the effect of spontaneously eliciting opportunities for commonality and sharing between client and therapist. In our experience, this becomes a unique dynamic tension, involving careful monitoring of the client's experience and an active ongoing attention to therapeutic boundaries, such as contract, confidentiality, time constraints, payment, etc., which are designed to support and protect the asymmetry (Jordan and Marshall 2010).

Attachment to nature

Attachment theory places the role of mother (or caregiver) as central to the infant's developing sense of self and emotional stability (Bowlby 1969, 1988; Stern 1985; Main 2000). Bowlby's original research into attachment has achieved worldwide recognition (Bowlby 1969). He proposed that we develop internal working models of attachment, ranging from secure to insecure, the subsets of which are avoidant, ambivalent and disorganised. Ainsworth developed these ideas further, subjecting them to experimental research, developing the strange situation experiment. The experiment looked at how an infant dealt with separation from their caregiver while in the presence of a stranger, and how attachment behaviour, secure, insecure and avoidant, could be seen in the infant's responses (Ainsworth 1978).

If we see attachment as manifest in patterns of behaviour, then we can explore how aspects of internal working models can be applied to relationships with nature. I will outline aspects of internal working models as defined by Main (2000). Securely attached individuals find it relatively easy to get close to others and are comfortable depending on people and having an interdependent relationship: they do not often worry about being abandoned or about someone getting too close to them. Those with avoidant attachment patterns are somewhat uncomfortable being close to others; they find it difficult to trust others completely and have difficulty allowing themselves to be dependent. The third style is anxious/ambivalent: those who find that others are reluctant to get as close as they would like and who often worry that their partner does not really love them or want to stay with them.

In some sense the dominant attachment pattern that industrialised societies have to nature is one of avoidance and ambivalence. Searles (1960: 6) makes a similar point, seeing relatedness to the non-human environment as one of the transcendentally important facts of human living, and the ambivalence we feel towards it, in the way we ignore its importance to us, as the source of problems in psychological well-being.

Shepard (1995), in his treatise 'Nature and madness', argues that most of us fail to become as mature as we could be, that we act on primitive fears and fantasies, located in our unconscious world yet acting as a driving force on our relationships both with each other and with the planet. In terms of development, Shepard argues that the shape of all otherness grows out of the maternal relationship. However, similar to Searles, he proposes that this relationship is formed within the backdrop of the environment that exists for both infant and mother. In the evolution of humankind this setting took the form of living plants, wild birds, rain, wind, mud and the taste and texture of earth and bark, the sounds of animals and insects. These surroundings were swallowed, internalised, incorporated as the self (Shepard 1995: 27). In terms of modern society, development for Shepard takes the form of an 'ontogenetic' crippling, adolescent narcissism, oedipal fears, ambivalence and inconsistency, all of which are projected out onto the environment. This historical march away from nature results in these private nightmares manifesting in broken climates and technologies which pursue an infantile sense of mastery, the upshot of which is ever-worsening problems.

These ideas so central to psychoanalysis (and latterly aspects of attachment theory) explain why the idea of dependency on the planet is so threatening to aspects of our sense of self. If complicated dependency issues are set up in infancy with the primary caregiver, these cannot help but become manifest in our relationship to the planet and nature. In this way an understanding of the human problem of need and dependency can help us more fully understand why we are in the current environmental mess and have developed an insecure, avoidant and ambivalent relationship to nature and the planet.

The importance of attachment in emotional regulation

The current environmental crisis powerfully reminds us of the fact that we are in relationship to the more-than-human world and that facets of this relationship are central to our concepts of self and the process of emotional regulation. The idea of a secure base is very important in attachment theory (Bowlby 1969; Ainsworth 1978). If we posit aspects of nature as both a maternal and paternal presence in our lives, an example can illustrate just how aspects of our well-being become intrinsically linked to natural environments. It is a quote from Roger Deakin, the British naturalist, on the death of his father:

> The day a policeman came to the door and told me my father had died might actually have been the moment that made me into a conservationist. I had lost such a big part of my life that I needed to compensate by holding on tightly to everything else. This may be the source of my passion for conservation.
>
> (Deakin 2008: 47)

From this perspective nature can be seen as representing a secure base, an aspect of both our internal and external relational world that can provide great comfort. Fonagy et al. (2002) present us with the idea of affect regulation, a process whereby the individual is able to maintain a regulatory position in relation to their own mood states, maximising positive and minimising negative mood states. This capacity is intrinsically linked to good attachments formed in early infancy which help the infant to regulate their own emotional mood states. I think there is strong evidence, especially from research in environmental psychology, to argue that people use natural environments in order to help them shift negative mood states and maintain positive ones.

In speaking of attachment we are talking of love. How can we love well? How can we speak of our loves? In some senses in taking the risk to love and become attached we are also acknowledging the inevitability of some form of loss. Nicholson (2003) says that in speaking of our love we bring our issues of dependency and vulnerability to the fore, as what is loved can be lost or harmed or can even betray us. Who has not had to turn away from the television or newspaper when some new image of the destruction of the natural world reminds us of how what we value can be taken away? We have to wrestle with our own feelings of powerlessness and helplessness.

Nature as a transitional object

Object relations theory, as espoused by writers such as Klein (1997) and Winnicott, can be seen as perhaps the first real attempt to articulate the emotional environment as important in the psychological and emotional development of the individual. Winnicott (1958) has articulated the idea of emotional space in early infant development. In his theory of transitional phenomena and transitional objects, he identifies the importance of the growing relationship to interior emotional and exterior emotional spaces for the baby. This process undertaken in relation to the mother and the outer world is where the baby is attempting to negotiate the relationship between the 'me' and the 'not me'. Winnicott sees the transitional phenomena that the baby is using as a way of the infant making sense of objects that are not part of the infant's body, yet are not fully recognised as belonging to external reality. He introduces the idea of the 'transitional space', a space between the dyad of inner and outer:

there is the third part of the life of a human being, a part that we cannot ignore, an intermediate area of experiencing, to which inner reality and external life both contribute. It is an area which is not challenged, because no claim is made on its behalf except that it shall exist a resting-place for the individual engaged in the perpetual human task of keeping inner and outer reality separate yet inter-related.

(Winnicott 1951: 230)

Winnicott introduces the idea of the space between the objective and subjective world of the infant; in fact the transitional space is a way of aiding the infant to negotiate this sense of the subjective and objective. He sees play as the vehicle through which the transitional space functions to both join and separate the baby and the mother. Winnicott falls back onto the interior of the infant, stating how external objects are appropriated and used in the service of emotional development, and used in the defence against anxiety and depressive states. Transitional objects in their symbolic form represent the 'external' breast – the good enough 'mother', who makes active adaption to the infant's needs, and helps the infant to negotiate the emotional upheavals of early emotional development (Winnicott 1951).

Counselling and psychotherapy from a psychodynamic perspective have always foregrounded the holding environment as the space within which affect can be understood and contained (Bion 1970). The holding environment and containment of the client's emotional states have become synonymous with the room: the indoor, comfortable, safe and warm space. This in turn has become synonymous with safe, ethical counselling and psychotherapy practice (Casement 1992).

The importance of the transitional space that Winnicott (1951) posits allows for the concept of emotional space which can exist between the internal and external, the subjective and objective, the mother and the infant. This helps us to start to imagine other forms of emotionality which can exist within and between geographical and relational 'spaces', and between mind and nature.

Case example

Duncan was a trainee solicitor; his previous experiences of therapy had been difficult, Duncan reporting that the therapist had put him in touch with feelings that were very difficult and that he didn't know what to do with. At assessment Duncan talked about his family history; his mother and father's marriage had been volatile and unstable with numerous splits and walkouts; his mother had been self-obsessed, using her children in a narcissistic way to meet her own needs. Duncan had grown up with a poor sense of himself, quite often adapting himself to others' needs and wishes in order to be liked. He was mistrustful and the therapist assessing him had a strong counter-transference feeling that he was attacking and persecuting Duncan through his questions. There were long pauses and silences in the subsequent sessions and Duncan reported feeling very ambivalent about therapy. The therapist suggested they might meet outdoors and walk together, as the sessions indoors felt so difficult, and for them both to see how this felt. They met on a beach and walked and talked by the sea. In the session Duncan talked more about how he felt and the session went well; at the end the therapist asked Duncan how he felt about this way of working. Duncan reported that he found it 'much easier' to talk without the room and the eye contact of the therapist and that compared to his previous experiences of therapy it was much easier to open up and share with the therapist outdoors whilst they were walking. In subsequent sessions they met in coastal locations and walked and talked. The therapist also found it easier to tune into Duncan on an embodied level and make contact with him more easily than he had done indoors. At times Duncan would stop and make eye contact with the therapist when he had a particularly important thing to say in therapy. As the sessions progressed, Duncan was more able to initiate contact in this way in the therapy and began to be more able to stay in touch with painful feelings whilst moving outdoors.

There are a number of things illustrated in this example about why for some clients working in an outdoor natural space allows them to make and maintain emotional contact with the therapist more easily. If we look at this through the lens of attachment theory initially, difficult early experiences of attachment and intimacy can lead to problems with an ability to emotionally regulate oneself. For some, the natural world forms a kind of 'good breast', a non-threatening and available other, who is alive and vibrant but at the same time much less invasive and threatening, more available and benign, than other attachments they may have. In this sense some clients may have grown up using nature in this way in order to help them emotionally regulate themselves, manage difficult attachments and negotiate proximity within intimate relationships. Even if this prior relationship to nature did not exist, we can see how, on a number of levels, nature can act as a mediating presence within therapy in order to help both therapist and client make and maintain contact with one another that feels manageable and less threatening. As feelings of safety and comfort grow in certain areas of the therapy, the client then becomes more able to negotiate difficult feelings and tolerate a greater intensity of intimacy with the therapist. Therapists themselves who are drawn to working in nature quite often have some attachment history with nature where they have used it in this way to negotiate more difficult experiences growing up, and we will look at this next as part of developing your own understanding of your therapeutic relationship with nature and how you may be able to begin to translate this into your therapeutic practice.

Concluding comments

In this chapter I have focused on the therapeutic relationship within an outdoor natural setting. I have proposed that the relational paradigm within psychotherapy offers a valuable way in which we can begin to understand certain aspects of the therapeutic relationship outdoors such as transference and counter transference as well as change processes. Giving case examples I have tried to illustrate how nature is an important variable in understanding and mitigating attachment patterns, and also the way nature may act as a transitional object helping to create a different form of emotional space between therapist and client that feels less threatening for clients who have had poor early relational experiences.

References

Ainsworth, M. (1978) *Patterns of Attachment: A Psychological Study of the Strange Situation*. Hillsdale, NJ: Lawrence Erlbaum Associates.

Berger, R. (2006) Beyond words: nature-therapy in action. *Journal of Critical Psychology, Counseling and Psychotherapy* 6(4), 195–199.

Bion, W. R. (1970) *Attention and Interpretation: A Scientific Approach to Insight in Psycho-analysis and Groups*. London: Tavistock Publications.

Boston Change Process Study Group (BCPSG) (2010) *Change in Psychotherapy: A Unifying Paradigm*. New York: Norton.

Bowlby, J. (1969) *Attachment and Loss*, vol. 1, *Attachment*. New York: Basic Books.

Bowlby, J. (1988) *A Secure Base: Clinical Applications of Attachment Theory*. London: Routledge.

Bridges, N. A. (1999) Psychodynamic perspective on therapeutic boundaries: creative clinical possibilities. *Journal of Psychotherapy Research and Practice* 8(4), 292–300.

Casement, P. (1992) *On Learning from the Patient*. Hove: Guilford Press.

Deakin, R. (2008) Call of the wild. *Guardian Weekend*, 25 October.

Fonagy, P., Gergely, G., Jurist, E. L. and Target, M. (2002) *Affect Regulation, Mentalization and the Development of the Self*. New York: Other Press.

Freud, S. (1912) The dynamics of transference. *Standard Edition 12*. London: Hogarth Press, 1958, pp. 97–108.

Gill, M. (1982) *Analysis of Transference*, vol. 1, *Theory and Technique*. Madison, CT: International Universities Press.

Heimann, P. (1950) On counter-transference. *International Journal of Psycho-Analysis* 31, 81–84.

Jordan, M. and Marshall, H. (2010) Taking therapy outside: deconstructing or reconstructing the therapeutic frame? *European Journal of Psychotherapy and Counselling* 12(4), 345–359.

Klein, M. (1997) *Envy and Gratitude: And Other Works 1946–1963*. (Intro. by H. Segal). London: Vintage.

Kohut, H. (1971) *How Does Analysis Cure?* Chicago: University of Chicago Press.

Main, M. (2000) The organised categories of infant, child, and adult attachment: flexible vs inflexible attention under attachment related stress. *Journal of the American Psychological Association* 48(4), 1055–1096.

Mitchell, S. (1988) *Relational Concepts within Psychoanalysis: An Integration*. Cambridge, MA: Harvard University Press.

Nicholson, S. W. (2003) *The Love of Nature and the End of the World: The Unspoken Dimensions of Environmental Concern*. Cambridge, MA: MIT Press.

Proctor, G. (2010) Boundaries or mutuality in therapy: is mutuality really possible or doomed from the start? *Psychotherapy and Politics International* 8, 44–58.

Sander, L. (1988) The event-structure of regulation in the neonate-caregiver system as a biological background for early organization of psychic structure. In A. Goldberg (ed.) *Frontiers in Self Psychology*. Hillsdale, NJ: Analytic Press, pp. 64–77.

Santostefano, S. (2004) *Child Therapy in the Great Outdoors: A Relational View*. London: Hillside Press.

Searles, H. (1960) *The Nonhuman Environment: In Normal Development and in Schizophrenia*. New York: International Universities Press.

Shepard, P. (1995) Nature and madness. In T. Roszak, A. Kanner and M. Gomes (eds) *Ecopsychology: Restoring the Earth and Healing the Mind*. London: Sierra Club Books.

Stern, D. (1985) *The Interpersonal World of the Infant: A View from Psychoanalysis and Developmental Psychology*. New York: Basic Books.

Stolorow, R. D. and Atwood, G. E. (1992) *Contexts of Being: The Intersubjective Foundations of Psychological Life*. Hillsdale, NJ: Analytic Press.

Winnicott, D. (1951) Transitional objects and transitional phenomena. In D. Winnicott (1958) *Collected Papers: Through Paediatrics to Psycho-Analysis*. London: Tavistock.

Winnicott, D. (1958) *Collected Papers: Through Paediatrics to Psycho-Analysis*. London: Tavistock.

Chapter 4

Understanding the range of therapeutic processes in nature

There is no one-size-fits-all therapeutic approach to working in nature, but a range of processes and different emphases on aspects of the therapeutic relationship, with both therapist and nature, that come into focus at different times and for different reasons, depending upon the rationale and focus of the therapy. This is, of course, aligned with the fact that each individual client is unique and may require a unique and idiosyncratic approach that cannot easily be fitted into a single model of nature-based therapy. However, I will attempt to map out a broad multifaceted way of working in nature that can happen on different levels, for different purposes and at different stages in relation to therapeutic focus.

In Chapter 3 we looked at the therapeutic relationship within a natural setting and ways of understanding this from a relational perspective. The overarching focus, when working therapeutically in a natural setting, is understanding the relationship between inner and outer processes. In Chapter 1, I explored the question 'what is nature?' The position I take is that nature is a vital, relational, unfolding dynamic process. It works at a number of different levels, has aspects that are material, essential to life, but it also has powerful psychological properties, in terms of the effects it has on human consciousness and well-being. It is fundamentally something that we are in relationship with on a spectrum of connection to disconnection. What I will explore in this chapter is how these different levels work therapeutically, beginning to outline a multifaceted working model. This will allow you to begin to think about how you might work thera-peutically in the outdoors, and start to link this into your own therapeutic modality, and explore the rationale for working outdoors and the types of clients and contexts that you might be working within.

I want to outline three levels of working therapeutically within a natural setting and then go on to explore these in more depth, describing specific therapeutic activities and processes that come into play at these different levels. These are the concepts of 'Participation', 'Projection' and finally 'Personal/Transpersonal' processes in nature. These overlap and in practice are not always so easily distinguished.

Participation

The therapeutic process as it unfolds in the natural space can take the form of active or passive participation. We have looked at the evidence from environmental psychology research which found that passive experiencing of nature can have very beneficial effects, such as Ulrich's classic research which showed that a view from a hospital window promoted faster post-surgery recovery (Ulrich 1984). This may also be true of a passive backdrop for the normal process of therapy. For example a therapy session can be set up in a natural setting with two chairs and conducted in largely the same way that it would be in the room, and this passive experiencing of the context will have beneficial effects for both therapist and client. Passive engagement might also include mindfulness and experiencing processes, which will be explored in more depth below when we look at participation as a therapeutic process in nature. Participation, as an important aspect of understanding therapeutic process in nature, looks at how we can participate and be present in a natural environment. We are engaged on a number of different levels in this participative process, with our bodies in an embodied participative process, our senses, such as sight, sound, touch and smell, and with our thoughts and feelings. I will begin by looking at more active participatory experiences in nature, starting with walking and talking as therapy.

Walk and talk therapy

An increasing number of therapists are taking their practice outdoors and walking with their clients whilst conducting therapy. Doucette (2004) outlines aspects of walk and talk therapy as walking outdoors whilst engaged in counselling. Walk and talk therapy happens outside of the usual confines of an office space. The psychotherapy happens for fifty minutes but in the setting of a park, woodland or other natural space, which the therapist and client can access and choose. Physical activity and the outdoors are the central focus of the therapy. In Doucette's research with adolescents, therapist and participants met over six weeks, once per week for 30–45 minutes of walking outdoors on school grounds. Participants discussed what had happened that week; they were also taught strategies during sessions, which included ways of managing stress and stressful situations, positive self-talk, mental imagery and other focusing techniques to reduce stress (Doucette 2004).

Extended wilderness trips

Another way of working more actively in nature is to take clients on extended wilderness trips and overnight camping. Drawing from ideas in wilderness therapy (Berman and Berman 1994; Moore and Russell 2002; Davies-Berman and Berman 2009), therapists take groups out into remote locations in order to both challenge their clients psychologically and also foster a deeper connection to the natural world. This is achieved through being in a location far removed from an urban

Figure 2 Camping on trip (Photo: Author)

setting. There are some unique process aspects to this sort of therapeutic work, such as how to hold the therapeutic frame alongside other processes such as cooking, sleeping and toileting, the physical safety of the group and the particular skill set of the therapist. This is largely to do with the issue of physical safety, and the competency of the therapist in managing not only the psychological and emotional process of the group and individuals, but also their physical safety in challenging environments.

A longer therapeutic trip into a more remote location allows the therapeutic work to deepen, and being immersed in a natural space which is more remote from human civilisation allows participants to really experience themselves in this terrain. Greenway (2009) believes that wilderness experiences can bring about dramatic psychological effects. Working with groups over a number of years he gathered data and stories about the changes participants experienced. He proposes that the wilderness effect works on a number of different levels or 'modes of knowing'. Initially participants' bodies are 'awakened' through the physicality of being outdoors and of carrying kit and equipment. Then a group process emerges whereby mutual support and caring are encouraged through sharing camp duties, cooking, and eating food together. Sharing dreams in the morning is important. During a wilderness trip the majority of decisions are made by group consensus.

Sitting around a fire and cooking awakens an archetypical connection to an earlier way of living and being. Toileting outside and managing your own waste also creates an intimacy with one's own body, and here the human–nature relationship becomes very personal. The geography of rivers and mountains is also important in deepening this connection and providing a wider sense of feeling connected to the earth. For Greenway the immersion in a wilderness experience allows for a deeper connection to nature and to the self.

Approaches such as the Natural Change Project (Key and Kerr 2011) utilise aspects of psychotherapy, especially in exploring emotional and group processes, in conjunction with ideas and practices from outdoor experiential education, to develop a greater awareness of our relationship to nature. Influenced by the ideas of deep ecology (Naess 1973) and ecopsychology (Roszak et al. 1995), the central aim of processes which immerse people in wilderness contexts for extended periods of time is to foster a greater sense of an ecological self, a self that sees itself as fundamentally connected to and part of the natural world. Although the approach is not exclusively psychotherapy, it represents a move towards a broader set of therapeutic goals which see personal distress as fundamentally linked to planetary distress and that these processes cannot easily be separated from one another.

Case example

A group participated in a five-day camping and walking trip in the mountains of Scotland. The purpose of the trip was to take themselves deeper into a wilderness location and to camp and journey through this landscape, exploring their sense of connection to the land and working on the personal and group issues that arose through engagement in this process. A central aspect of the trip was preparation and engagement in a twelve-hour solo experience, whereby individuals left their camp at dawn to sit and be in a solo spot (which they had already found and agreed upon with the group facilitators) until dusk, when they would return to the camp in silence until the next morning, when they would share their experiences and be helped to integrate their learning from this.

Although solo experiences in wilderness locations have the potential to be very powerful, I want to sound a note of caution around extended wilderness trips which can quite often result in profound psychological change, which is the importance of the return to urban civilisation. The danger is that the wilderness experience is like a psychological 'one-night stand' with nature, which results in a peak experience but which may not be translatable to that person's life and situation when they return to the urban setting from which they came, which they may now see as 'all wrong'. The key to experiences like this is how they are incorporated into a person's life and, if they are part of a psychotherapeutic process, how the learning from this experience can be understood in the context of their emotional life and relationships.

Mindfulness processes in nature

One of the ways we can begin to start noticing what is going on for us when we arrive in a natural setting is to 'tune' in to both an inner process and an outer sense of where we are. One of the easiest ways to do this is through focused attention, and this can be achieved through mindfulness exercises. Mindfulness, as an important therapeutic tool, has been widely written about in recent years, especially in the treatment of depression (Williams et al. 2007). There are different interpretations of mindfulness, but as a concept it can be linked to Buddhist psychology and can be seen as a way of focusing attention and becoming more aware (Mace 2007). Altschuler (2004) wrote a book on hiking and mindfulness, walking the sky trail on the Pacific coast. Within the book there are some interesting stories and guided exercises to develop self-awareness through walking and being mindful. Mindfulness can be used as a way of allowing people to arrive and then to slow down and begin to focus on where they are and what might be going on. Mindfulness, as a way of beginning a session with a client or group, can also be useful in marking a transition into a different internal space. The following extract illustrates how mindfulness was used in order to allow clients to centre themselves and start to focus in a different way.

Figure 3 Carved stone figure at breathing space (Photo: Author)

Case example

A group was coming for a day exploring the therapeutic potential of nature. They were walking from a meeting point (a car park) to where the workshop was going to take place. There was a lot of chatter and talking, so before they set off the facilitator gently asked them to stop talking. She then asked them to become more aware of their breathing and then to begin to follow her as she walked to the workshop site; she also asked them to gently begin to notice how their bodies felt when moving and any aches, pains, etc. It was a cold winter's day so she also suggested they become aware through their senses of the feel of the air on their skin and also notice any sounds. The group quite quickly entered into a softer and quieter space as they arrived at the site; she then asked them to sit and to continue noticing the relationship between their inner and outer experience. This exercise or something similar can also be done for individual clients at the beginning of a session where you may either be sitting or walking and talking.

Focusing in nature

Focusing in nature specifically draws upon Gendlin's notion of 'felt sense' (Gendlin 1996); this is an embodied way of knowing, drawing upon and gradually focusing in on, felt sensations within the body. Harris (2013) proposes that 'felt sense' can allow us to access a vast amount of information about our environment, breaking down dualities between subjectivity and objectivity, mind and nature, which allows new and creative ways of forming intersubjective relations between humans, and humans and the more-than-human world.

Focusing can be used in nature to gain a great awareness of how inner processes relate to an outer reality. Schroeder (2008) has used focusing in natural environments to gain a greater awareness of felt sense in certain natural spaces. Schroeder says:

> When I am in a natural environment, I pay attention to what I am feeling inside and how that is affected by my surroundings. I almost always notice a definite change in my feelings after I have spent a little while in a natural place. I try to observe what is happening inside me and then sense what it is about the environment and situation that is bringing forth such a change. I sometimes then have openings of insight into how and why a natural environment enables this change to occur. I find words or phrases that express these insights and check them against the felt sense to see if there is a resonance or response that confirms the rightness of that way of expressing the insight. Sometimes this develops into a kind of mini-theory that both explains and carries forward my sense of nature and how I respond inwardly to natural surroundings.
>
> (2008: 64)

Schroeder (2008) sees nature as an 'egoless other' and, in a theory that echoes attention restoration theory, aspects of Jungian thought and process theories of nature, says it is the fact that we are both part of nature and separate from it due to culture that gets in the way of our ability to feel part of nature. Through deliberate focusing activities in natural settings we can tune in and begin to feel, starting from the place of personal experience in order to feel nature and a greater sense of connection.

Engagement with the senses

Another way to participate in the natural environment is to walk out into the space and to begin to notice on a number of different levels how our senses are engaged. One of the ways this can be achieved is to ask the individual and/or the group to go out with the intent to notice, on a number of different levels, how the natural space 'feels'. This can be done through engagement with their bodies, their senses or their feelings. For example people might want to take their shoes off and walk barefoot; they might want to seek out smells and make sensual contact with the plant life, or other aspects of the natural space where they are – this might be water or contact with soil.

There are a number of different exercises and books written on this process of participative reconnection to nature. Drawing from ideas in Gestalt therapy, Swanson (2001) advocates that discovery is the most powerful form of learning, which leads to a greater awareness. This happens not just through your thoughts but through your feelings and perceptions. Swanson outlines a number of activities in nature which will allow a greater depth of experiencing and connection, explore a more intimate I–Thou connection to nature, and help expand the boundaries of self.

Abram talks about the importance of sensuous engagement in his book *The Spell of the Sensuous* (1996). Through the senses he argues we can begin to locate ourselves again within the wider ecological matrix of which we are a part. Of central importance is the link between interior mental process and an outer awareness via contact with the 'sensorial field'. Abram says this is the contact of the human body with the animate earth:

> By acknowledging such links between the inner, psychological world and the perceptual terrain that surrounds us, we begin to turn inside-out, loosening our psyche from its confinement within a strictly human sphere, freeing sentience to return to the sensible world that contains us. Intelligence is no longer ours alone but it is a property of the earth; we are in it, of it immersed in its depths.
>
> (1996: 262)

Embodied process

The body has a central role in making contact with nature and the elements in outdoor work. Because of this we need to think about the participation of the body in nature-based therapy. In the case example given in Chapter 3 the client got in touch with an embodied process that allowed access to a moment of meeting, subsequently opening up a different way of relational knowing. Nature-based therapy offers a way to both access and work with the body–mind relationship and the emotions associated with this.

Frizell (2008) says the body is a dynamic organism which connects us with the outer processes of the world, and the body responds to stimuli from inside and outside acting as a central conduit through which we can mediate an exchange between the inside and outside. Beauvais (2012) sees the relationship between the body and wider systems of ecosystemic health as central to understanding human–nature relationships. The body may somatically represent different forms of distress which are both emotional and environmental; quite often as we have become split off from nature we have also become split off from our bodies.

Case example

After exploring the statement that she 'hated her body' my client and I discussed ways in which she could begin to gently reconnect to her body in a supportive and friendly way. We discussed alternative therapies such as yoga but my client stated she disliked all forms of alternative medicine and body-oriented approaches. She did however like walking in nature and we jointly agreed that she would start to walk in nature between sessions and begin to focus on her felt sense of her body and start to shift her relationship by talking to her body in more warm and supportive ways. We also agreed for her to begin sensory awareness activities, using smell and touch, to start a process of reconnection to her surroundings and check in, using her felt sense, how this felt in her body.

Burns (2012) sees the relationship between humans and the more-than-human world as embodied. Foregrounding ideas from attachment theory and object relations she proposes that somatic communication can go on between bodies and bodies, and bodies and environments. These emergent phenomena can be explored within the relational contexts of movers and witnesses, using the idea of 'kinaesthetic empathy' (Pallaro 2007) which involves embodying a client's feeling states and movement qualities by the therapist.

Case example

A client and her therapist were following a trail through a forest; as the session progressed the therapist was aware of a growing sense of urgency in her body and a need to move more quickly as though she was trying to outrun something. This was coupled with a sense of embodied anxiety she experienced in her stomach and in her legs. She shared this sense with the client by asking whether the client felt anxious and had a need to 'run away'. The client said yes, it was exactly what she had been struggling with in the session after a particularly difficult week.

The relationship between natural space and therapeutic effect

Several therapists I interviewed in my research discussed how certain geographic spaces possessed particular qualities that were conducive to conducting therapeutic work. This highlights an interesting link between space and affect, and how geographical places and spaces have an affect on emotions and can be deliberately used in therapy in order to facilitate the exploration of emotions and feeling responses. Certain natural locations can be felt to have particular internal resonances; for example woodland can be seen to have a holding and containing emotional effect, so that for some woodland is in and of itself a therapeutic space. For others more liminal spaces such as coastlines and beaches, which are situated between the land and sea, may have a powerful emotional resonance which can be explored therapeutically. This process is magnified when working in more remote locations with groups, whereby particular wilderness locations, such as mountains, can be used in order to facilitate a deeper connection with the natural world and to provoke particular internal emotional and psychological responses, in order for these to be explored therapeutically.

These emotional geographies (Bondi et al. 2005) are very important for therapeutic work outdoors and link to several books written within a literary framework which articulate the powerful emotional resonance of place and space in the outdoors. Nan Shepard illustrates this very well in talking about her solo trips in the Cairngorms:

> It is a journey into Being: for as I penetrate more deeply into the mountain's life, I penetrate also into my own. For an hour I am beyond desire. It is not ecstasy, that leaps out of oneself that makes man like a god. I am not out of myself, but in myself. I am. To know being, that is the final grace accorded from the mountain.
>
> (1996: 6)

The following case example illustrates the deliberate use of natural space for therapeutic process.

Case example

A therapist was working with a group over a weekend in the mountains of North Wales. They had been walking in the hills in windy and wet weather; the therapist felt they needed to stop and process how they were feeling, but felt strongly that doing this in an exposed location would feel too emotionally as well as physically exposing and that therapeutically it wouldn't allow the group to feel 'held' at all. So she chose a bowl-shaped area which had trees and some natural shelter from the wind and rain. The group stopped here and when they had made themselves comfortable with a warm drink and something to eat she asked them how they were feeling and what had come up for them in the walk.

The therapeutic rationale for participative experiences within nature is to encourage clients to awaken their senses. This is in order to address overall patterns of relationality and to feel a connection with the more-than-human world. In doing this, part of the effect is to reawaken and understand human connections at the same time and how relationships take on different forms and have different feeling qualities. In nature-guided therapy (Burns 1998) clients are given sensual awareness tasks, such as watching a sunset, in order to discover a range of emotional responses which are available to the client; these can then be brought back into the therapy and worked with.

In using nature in conjunction with mindfulness and focusing activities, the therapeutic rationale aligns itself with the 'third wave' of psychological therapies, which aim to work more with acceptance and understanding than with problem solving. Clients can begin to become more aware of their inner feeling states and how these relate to outer awareness and relationships. Nature forms the perfect backdrop and context within which to gently explore one's self and one's senses; as a vital dynamic process it can serve to enliven the senses.

Next I will look at the rich variety of metaphors that nature provides and how these can act as a projective screen and mirror through which the client can gain access to different aspects and patterns of relationships.

Projection

Projection, as a mechanism, originates from object relations theorist Melanie Klein. She posited projection as a process the infant undertook in order to negotiate the relationship between inner and outer reality. Klein (Mitchell 1986) believed that the baby was attempting to get rid of unwanted feelings and locate them in the mother; this was in order that the mother could identify and understand the feelings (projective identification) and in so doing offer the feelings back to the infant in a more manageable form. Projection from this perspective allows a person to attempt to manage a difficult inner reality, such as feelings of anger or anxiety, by projecting the feelings outwards, normally towards a person, object or idea. This might take the form of saying someone else seems angry when it may be difficult to own your own angry feelings. Projection as a mechanism allows us to gain access to inner reality by using the outer world as a place where we may be able to understand our feelings more clearly.

In working with projection in natural spaces we are foregrounding the importance of inner reality and touching upon one of the central ideas in psychotherapy. Here we are coming up against a tension around more language-based approaches that have an emphasis on symbolic reality and the more sensual experiential components of nature-based therapy, and the argument that language may get in the way of a connection to nature and act as a distancing process.

Arts therapies and nature

Creative arts therapies have used projection as a central therapeutic mechanism with which to work creatively with feelings in therapy. Using the object of art (be it music, drama or image), feelings can be worked at and reintegrated at a safe distance from the person. Projection may also be twofold in arts therapies, in that it can be located in both the art and the therapist. Indeed arts therapy approaches share a lot of commonalities with nature-based therapies and a lot of arts therapists have begun to utilise the natural world as a medium within which to work, finding this shift not as difficult as other talk-based therapists have found it, due to their training and working with symbolism.

The natural world may offer a lot of opportunities for externalising things, allowing somebody to get things outside of their head and to be able to experience them in a number of different ways in the natural space. The natural world offers a rich variety of natural materials and processes to work with therapeutically. Farrelly-Hanson (2001) sees art therapy and nature as working together in a healing process where creativity and living processes become intertwined and operate to alleviate distress and promote well-being.

Case example

A client and therapist had decided to go to the beach as part of their session; they had discussed how to explore the client's difficulty with accepting life's ups and downs as part of an ongoing process. The sea acted as a perfect metaphor through which they could explore the incoming and outgoing tides of life. The client was encouraged to work with stones that they found on the beach and to name them as difficulties they were struggling with. The client decided to build a stone mandala and then to watch as the waves washed over it, working with the feelings that arose from this.

If therapy is linked to living processes that occur within natural settings, it seems to have the potential for a more powerful effect and can be seen to challenge the idea that emotions exist primarily as an inner experience. Ingold (2011) takes this point further by stating that cognitive psychology struggles to see how action cannot be preceded by interior mental representation, that intention has to be conceived in thought. Ingold posits something else – that action becomes immanent to a living dynamic relational field. In this sense, and drawing from Deleuze and Guattari (1977, 1988), we can see how thought in relation to nature becomes immanent and unfolding, a dynamic living interaction with vibrant matter (Bennet 2010). If we then relate this to therapy and therapeutic process, the interaction within the dynamic unfolding event that is the natural world has a powerful therapeutic effect.

Figure 4 Art making in nature (Photo: Author)

Importance of metaphor

Located more in the work of adventure therapy and outward bound, Bacon (1983) sees the rich opportunity for metaphor in working outdoors. He posits the concept of isomorphic and non-isomorphic metaphors originating from his work in outward bound. An isomorphic metaphor is the idea that a living and enacted metaphor for someone's life can be carried out and explored in therapeutic work in an outdoor natural space. In this sense a metaphor becomes a living enacted process. It might be that somebody is struggling with a sense of conflict in their relationship, and in working more actively with the living metaphor of conflict and cooperation a different outcome can be gained. For example, in his psychotherapeutic work Nick Ray took a couple, who were experiencing relationship difficulties, rock climbing. In this process they had to explore issues of trust and conflict within a living framework of ropes and rock, which allowed the dynamic between them to come more alive and be worked with explicitly in the process of therapy 'on the rock face' (Richards 2005).

Ronen Berger's 'Nature Therapy' draws on approaches originating in the arts therapies, so it is not surprising his work uses and works with a lot of metaphor and imagery. In the approaches he uses, such as 'building a home in nature', clients are encouraged to work with materials they find in nature to construct this space, which is then explored in relation to current issues in their life. Symbolism and metaphor are central to this therapeutic process in nature. Similarly, Linden and Grut (2002) see several processes that unfold within working in a garden environment as containing metaphors for the human condition, whereby the client's inner world is reflected back and encountered in natural metaphors which can directly relate to issues a client may be currently struggling with.

We can also see how Santostefano's (2004) concept of embodied life metaphors brings together the concept of metaphor and embodiment in working outdoors. In working through trauma with children Santostefano gives several examples of enactive movement and contact with nature. The child can represent internal psychological difficulties through enactments with spaces such as caves, hills and so forth, and this is mirrored by the therapist who registers and conveys through visceral responses, such as gasp or change of posture, in order to convey understanding of the child's unformulated emotional experience.

Personal/transpersonal process

The personal/transpersonal element of nature-based therapy highlights the meaning that the natural world gives to our lives and existence. For some this may be on a personal and spiritual level (transpersonal), or it may be through contact with the seasons and seasonal processes, an understanding of ourselves within a process that feels much greater than ourselves (existential). It may also be understood through a personal commitment to addressing the environmental crisis, species extinction and other aspects of environmental concern. Nature-based therapies that are informed by ecopsychology may be driven by a rationale that challenges societal norms, addressing what some see as the madness of industrialised capitalism. However these dimensions and their importance will be different and unique for each person approaching the field and wanting to understand more about their relationship with the natural world. Connecting to nature for some allows them to connect with a much deeper part of themselves and their spirituality in a broad sense. Historically, indigenous societies lived much more in tune with the seasons and processes of nature, largely because they had to in order to survive and bring in the harvest, etc. This intimate connection forged a way of understanding nature and the meaning and role it played in their lives.

Aboriginal culture existed for at least 40,000 years unchanged prior to colonisation by European settlers. It is a culture so intrinsically linked to the land that what the Aboriginal saw (and still sees) was not an environment with different geographical aspects, but a profoundly metaphysical landscape capable of expressing their deepest spiritual yearnings. The sacred landscape, framed within the confines of the church or cathedral walls for the European, existed for the Aboriginal as open space, trees, rocks and rivers, central to well-being and happiness. From this perspective the land becomes iconic in its essence, not only a container in its purely physical attributes but in terms of its metaphysical qualities. This web of systemic connections becomes central to the idea of land as self and can also be seen in Celtic and Norse mythologies – known in one form as the 'web of wyrd', the interconnectivity between all things, human and more-than-human (Bates 1992).

Working with the seasons

Working with seasonal processes is one way of connecting to a greater sense of our connection to nature and how we exist within a web of interconnection. In his book *Environmental Arts Therapy and the Tree of Life* (2009), Ian Siddons-Heginworth uses the cycles of nature, months of the year, Celtic and Greek mythology and creative arts therapy approaches to weave together a way of working therapeutically within nature that incorporates myth, metaphor and the wheel of the year to explore personal journeys within therapy. The use of nature as a seasonal process offers rich opportunities to explore the changing cycles of life and death, birth and renewal, to see ourselves as connected to a much greater whole, and the resultant feelings that arise from this.

The idea of the self as existing within a seasonal process reflects back the idea that we are not static in terms of our state of mind or our ability to transcend difficulties. We are always in a process of change and transition from one season to the next. This idea has been used in lifespan psychology to understand the seasons of a person's life (Levinson 1978). Moving around a wheel of self allows us to connect with a wider process in nature – of death, birth, growth and renewal. These are seen as inescapable facts of a nature-based psychology.

Case example

A group of cancer patients were working with a therapist in a woodland setting. They were at different stages of their experience with cancer but were all facing the potential of their illness being terminal. At the time of the year they were moving into autumn. Gathered around a warm fire, the therapist shared the story of 'Persephone'. The story tells of how Persephone came to spend time in the underworld and in particular when she bids farewell to her mother Demeter on earth, and takes her pomegranate (which contains all of earth's fertile seasonal seeds) below ground to spend the next half of the year with her husband in Hades. The story offers a rich metaphor for gathering our own personal harvest and the balance between light and dark at this time of the year. The group were then asked to move out into the woods and bring back natural objects which told of their own journey and harvest in life and how they might prepare to go into the underworld.

Working with the four directions in nature

The 'four shields' psychology, developed by Steven Foster and Meredith Little (1998), is based on the Native American tradition of the medicine wheel; the four directions correspond with the four points of the compass and the four seasons.

They also represent aspects of our psychological make-up and the stages of maturity that the participant is seeking to pass through in a journey of transition. The 'four shields' shares a kinship with ancient psychology where there was no differentiation between people and nature, where human life was intimately tied into the seasonal changes. South is summer; the psychological aspect is of childhood and bodily sensation, instinct, urge, desire and lust. West is autumn; the psychological aspect is of adolescence, introspection – emotions such as fear and self-doubt may be present in this shield. It is a place of initiation when the child of summer is preparing to become the adult of winter. The north is winter; the psychological aspect is of adulthood, mind, design and order. The adult of winter must do what needs to be done to survive, to store food for the long dark nights of winter, to make sure there is enough fuel for warmth. Finally the adult makes the transition to the east, which is spring. The psychological state is a reflection of the other shields, manifest in wisdom and the position of 'elder' but also paradoxically of infant and rebirth. It is the state of insight, spirituality and healing (Foster and Little 1998).

Case example

I was engaged with a group exploring personal transitions from student to qualified health professional. The setting was a mountainous area in Wales where the group were camping over a weekend. The group participated in a number of exercises, moving around a wheel of self, comprising the four directions: north, east, south and west. After one exercise where participants were instructed to walk in the direction of the south and reflect upon their childhood experiences, a participant returned with this account: 'I came to an area of vegetation where a dry bush had been burnt in a fire. From the ashes new growth was emerging, looking much healthier than before, with more nutrients from the ashes starting to sustain new growth. I took from this encounter a metaphor of my difficult childhood: growing up in a barren environment, the product of an unhappy marriage, an experience that had "burnt" me in a similar way to the bushes being burnt. My interest in psychology and therapy was largely a result and an attempt, as I suspect of all therapists, to heal myself. I wondered whether I had to feel pain again to grow, to heal – seeking nutrients from the ashes of my experience.'

(from Jordan 2009)

Foster and Little (1983, 1989, 1992, 1998) have developed their work around the 'four shields' from years of running vision quests. Therapeutic work in nature from this perspective focuses on the process of the vision quest as a mechanism of psychological change. Their work draws from rites-of-passage models known to traditional cultures as ways of negotiating life stages (Van Gennep 1960). The modern-day vision quest advocated by Foster and Little (1983) places the individual within a wilderness environment, without food or shelter, for a solitary three- or four-day experience of aloneness. This experience is then shared with others in a group process in order to make meaning and gain a 'vision' or life purpose that is contextualised as part of a process of transition for that individual. I myself participated in an experience such as this (Jordan 2005) and suffered from a profound depression subsequent to returning from the process. The vision quest process within psychotherapy needs to be treated with caution due to its extremes of hunger and isolation. However, the need to set up reconnective processes with natural phenomena is arguably vital to both emotional and mental well-being and forms a strong thread within transpersonal reconnective ideas and practice.

The importance of working with ritual

Another important aspect of working in nature from a transpersonal perspective is the use of ritual in facilitating therapeutic change. Ritual has been used for centuries in order to reconnect the self with something deeper and more sacred, and through this to come to some understanding of the greater meaning of suffering and crisis in our lives, and to find a way through this. Ritual allows us to feel less isolated and to feel a greater connection to something beyond ourselves. In a sense psychotherapy has always been imbued with rituals that need not always connect with something sacred, for example certain ways of greeting, speaking and even the location of the chairs in a room (Chandler 2010). Other writers have positioned the sacred within ritual as an important part of its healing power within psychotherapy (Cole 2003; Bewley 1995).

Nature seems to offer a perfect backdrop in order to be able to connect to this sense of sacred and to use the potential power of this in order to facilitate healing. Jung believed that the loss of emotional participation in nature resulted in man feeling isolated in the cosmos. For Jung, matter was the tangible exterior of things and spirit the non-visible interior; ritual within nature can be a powerful way of bringing inner and outer reality together because nature for Jung is also imbued with spirit (Jung 1989). The use of ritual to negotiate difficult passages of life and to create a bridge between inner and outer reality has been present in religions and myths across the ages, and Campbell (1949) proposes that the rights of initiation teach the lesson of the essential oneness of the individual and the universe. He also views the ceremonial as submission to the inevitability of destiny. He outlined the 'monomyth' of the hero's journey, containing a three-stage process of separation, initiation and return, echoed in stories throughout the centuries and seen in the story of *Star Wars*, which George Lucas based on Campbell's ideas (Campbell and Moyers 1989).

I want to discuss the importance of the use of threshold or liminal space within nature-based therapy as an important aspect of a therapeutic process which utilises ritual. The creation of a certain kind of space within nature-based therapy is an important facet in its healing potential. Mircea Eliade, a scholar of religion and mythology, wrote about the importance of setting up sacred space in order to facilitate the process of religious ritual and belief, and to demarcate this space from the profane of everyday life (Eliade 1961). The tradition of healing space and ritual can be traced back to the Asklepian healing temples; utilised in Ancient Greece as spaces for holistic healing, they were often situated in beautiful spots and focused on both bodily and psychic healing (Kearney 2009).

Case example

Marion was grieving after the sudden and unexpected death of her husband after a short illness. The therapy was about supporting her to be with this awful event. After some weeks of talking about the emotional and practical difficulties she was experiencing every day (the couple had two young children), Marion decided she wanted to mark the end of one phase of her life – it had been a year since the death – and to begin to move on into a new sense of her future as a widow. She chose a particular space by the sea (the sea was an important element as it represented the tides of life) and created a ritual fire where she would burn some old documents relating to the past. Once the fire had burnt down she would then step across a threshold, a line she had created from ashes from the fire, into the next phase of her life. The therapist acted as a witness to this process and afterwards they sat and talked about how she felt.

The unconscious, psyche and nature

Jung positions the unconscious as a dynamic vital force which exists beyond consciousness. Sitting in relationship to our conscious ego, Jung describes the unconscious as a rhizome, a root-like structure that works below consciousness making dynamic connections between things. It compensates for the one-sidedness of the ego and rational consciousness; the unconscious from this perspective is seen as akin to nature, a natural force (Jung 1989). In this sense it is part of a vital unfolding relational dynamic that integrates us at a deeper level with the natural world and forces that are contained within it.

The therapeutic relationship, with both nature and the therapist, creates a vessel or a container for therapeutic change to occur. A key to this is the concept of 'space', which has been termed in contemporary psychotherapy as a 'third area'. Moving beyond the idea of life as consisting of an inner and outer dimension we need to think about an intermediate realm that exists between inner and outer (Schwartz-Salant 1998). The idea that the psyche exists solely within the individual is challenged: Hillman (1995) argues that the unconscious and the psyche are both partly psychic, partly material as a place where psyche and matter merge. Hillman proposes that the psyche is very much affected by the spaces it exists within:

> The 'bad' place I am 'in' may refer not only to a depressed mood or an anxious state of mind; it may refer to a sealed-up office tower where I work, a set-apart suburban subdivision where I sleep, or the jammed freeway on which I commute between the two.
>
> (1995: xx)

A Jungian perspective draws upon ideas from alchemy, which was based on the belief in the fundamental unity of all processes within nature: all of nature originates from a single substance, which is driven by the conflict of opposites. These opposites are held together by an overriding unity as the force driving the universe onwards, for example the relationship between masculine and feminine. The demise of alchemy and its emphasis on imaginal thinking and fantastic imagery was driven by the growth of rational science and the need to establish cause and effect (Schwartz-Salant 1998). Schwartz-Salant says that in essence alchemy is about transformation, and that change is the interaction between subject and object in which both are transformed (1998: 11).

Working from a transpersonal perspective in nature positions the possibilities for therapeutic change within a deeper and more profound connection between mind and matter; in doing so breaking down dualities between the self and nature:

> At times I feel as if I am spread out over the landscape and inside things, and am myself living in every tree, in the splashing of the waves, in the clouds and the animals that come and go, in the procession of the seasons.
>
> (Jung 1989: 225)

Concluding comments

In this chapter I have looked at three central concepts in understanding therapeutic process in nature. Participation in either active or passive forms helps us to understand how the experience of nature can be therapeutic on a number of levels and how participative processes can be utilised for therapeutic purposes. I then explored how projective processes, in particular the use of arts and metaphors, can be utilised to explore therapeutic material when conducting therapy outdoors. Finally I looked at the importance of both personal and transpersonal processes, how these link to seasonal processes and a deeper spiritual engagement with nature that can have a powerful therapeutic effect. One of the key things to consider when understanding therapeutic process in natural settings is that emotions are not purely located *within* people but exist *between* them. So the emotional space of therapy, i.e. where it is conducted, can become as important for the therapeutic process as anything else that goes on.

References

Abram, D. (1996) *The Spell of the Sensuous.* New York: Vintage.

Altschuler, S. (2004) *The Mindful Hiker: On the Trail to Find the Path.* Camarillo, CA: DeVorss.

Bacon, S. (1983) *The Conscious Use of Metaphor in Outward Bound.* Denver: Outward Bound.

Bates, B. (1992) *The Way of Wyrd*, 2nd edn. New York: HarperCollins.

Beauvais, J. (2012) Focusing on the natural world: an ecosomatic approach to attunement with an ecological facilitating environment. *Body, Movement and Dance Psychotherapy: An International Journal for Theory, Research and Practice* 7(4), 277–291.

Bennet, J. (2010) *Vibrant Matter: A Political Ecology of Things*. Durham, NC: Duke University Press.

Berman, J. and Berman, D. (1994) *Wilderness Therapy: Foundations Theory and Research*. Iowa: Kendall Hunt.

Bewley, A. (1995) Re-membering spirituality: use of sacred ritual in psychotherapy. *Women & Therapy* 16(2/3), 201–213.

Bondi, L., Davidson, J. and Smith, M. (2005) Introduction: geography's 'emotional turn'. In J. Davidson, L. Bondi and M. Smith (eds) *Emotional Geographies*. Aldershot: Ashgate.

Burns, A. (2012) Embodiment and embedment: integrating dance/movement therapy, body psychotherapy, and ecopsychology. *Body, Movement and Dance Psychotherapy: An International Journal for Theory, Research and Practice* 7(1), 39–54.

Burns, G. (1998) *Nature Guided Therapy: Brief Integrative Strategies for Health and Well-Being*. London: Taylor & Francis.

Campbell, J. (1949) *The Hero with a Thousand Faces*. Princeton, NJ: Princeton University Press.

Campbell, J. and Moyers, B. (1989) *The Power of Myth*. New York: Bantam Doubleday.

Chandler, K. (2010) In practice – ritual in psychotherapy. *Therapy Today* 21(10), 27–28.

Cole, V. L. (2003) Healing principles: a model for the use of ritual in psychotherapy. *Counselling and Values* 47(3), 184–194.

Davies-Berman, J. and Berman, D. (2009) *The Promise of Wilderness Therapy*. Association of Experiential Education.

Deleuze, G. and Guattari, F. (1977/2004) *Anti-Oedipus: Capitalism and Schizophrenia*. Trans. R. Hurley, M. Seem and H. R. Lane. London: Continuum.

Deleuze, G. and Guattari, F. (1988) *A Thousand Plateaus: Capitalism and Schizophrenia*. Trans. B. Massumi. London: Continuum.

Doucette, P. A. (2004) Walk and Talk: an intervention for behaviourally challenged youths. *Adolescence* 39(154), 373–388.

Eliade, M. (1961) *The Sacred and the Profane: The Nature of Religion*. New York: Harcourt.

Farrelly-Hanson, M. (2001) Nature: art therapy in partnership with the earth. In M. Farrelly-Hanson (ed.) *Spirituality and Art Therapy: Living the Connection*. London: Jessica Kingsley.

Foster, S. and Little, M. (1983) *The Trail to the Sacred Mountain: A Vision Fast Handbook for Adults*. Big Pine, CA: Lost Borders Press.

Foster, S. and Little, M. (1989) *The Roaring of The Sacred River: The Wilderness Quest for Vision and Self Healing*. Big Pine. CA: Lost Borders Press.

Foster, S. and Little, M. (1992) *The Book of The Vision Quest: Personal Transformation in The Wilderness*. New York: Fireside Books.

Foster, S. and Little, M. (1998) *The Four Shields: The Initiatory Seasons of Human Nature*. Big Pine, CA: Lost Borders Press.

Frizell, C. (2008) In search of the wider self. *e-motion* 18(1), 1–8.

Gendlin, E. T. (1996). *Focusing-Oriented Psychotherapy*. New York: Guilford Press.

Greenway, R. (2009) The wilderness experience as therapy: we've been here before. In L. Buzzell and C. Chalquist (eds) *Ecotherapy – Healing with Nature in Mind*. San Francisco: Sierra Club.

Harris, A. (2013) Gendlin and ecopsychology: focusing in nature. *Person-Centered and Experiential Psychotherapies* 12(4), 330–343.

Hillman, J. (1995) A psyche the size of the earth: a psychological foreword. In T. Roszak, M. Gomes and A. Kanner (eds) *Ecopsychology: Restoring the Earth, Healing the Mind.* London: Sierra Club.

Ingold, T. (2011) *Being Alive: Essays on Movement Knowledge and Description.* London: Routledge.

Jordan, M. (2005) The vision quest: a transpersonal process. Paper presented to the British Psychological Society Transpersonal Psychology Section Conference, 17 September 2005.

Jordan, M. (2009) Back to nature. *Therapy Today* 20(3), 26–28.

Jung, C. G. (1989) *Memories, Dreams and Reflections.* New York: Knopf.

Kearney, M. (2009) *A Place of Healing: Working with Nature and Soul at the End of Life.* New Orleans: Spring Journal Books.

Key, D. and Kerr, M. (2011) *The Natural Change Project: Catalysing Leadership for Sustainability.* World Wildlife Fund Scotland.

Levinson, D. (1978) *The Seasons of a Man's Life.* New York: Knopf.

Linden, S. and Grut, J. (2002) *The Healing Fields: Working with Psychotherapy and Nature to Rebuild Shattered Lives.* London: Frances Lincoln.

Mace, C. (2007) Mindfulness in psychotherapy: an introduction. *Advances in Psychiatric Treatment* 13, 147–154.

Mitchell, J. (1986) *The Selected Melanie Klein.* London: Penguin Books.

Moore, T. and Russell, K. (2002) *Studies of the Use of Wilderness for Personal Growth, Therapy, Education, and Leadership Development: An Annotation and Evaluation.* University of Idaho Wilderness Research Centre College of Natural Resources, University of Idaho, USA.

Naess, A. (1973) The shallow and the deep, long range ecology movement. A summary. *Inquiry* 16, 95–100.

Pallaro, P. (2007) Somatic countertransference: the therapist in relationship. In P. Pallaro (ed.) *Authentic Movement: Moving the Body, Moving the Self, Being Moved: A Collection of Essays*, vol. 2. Philadelphia, PA: Jessica Kingsley, pp. 176–193.

Richards, K. (2005) Transactions on the rock face. *Therapy Today* 16(10), 16–18.

Roszak, T., Gomes, M. and Kanner, A. (1995) *Ecopsychology: Restoring the Earth, Healing the Mind.* London: Sierra Club.

Sander, L. (1988) The event-structure of regulation in the neonate-caregiver system as a biological background for early organization of psychic structure. In A. Goldberg (ed.) *Frontiers in Self Psychology.* Hillsdale, NJ: Analytic Press, pp. 64–77.

Santostefano, S. (2004) *Child Therapy in the Great Outdoors: A Relational View.* London: Hillside Press.

Schroeder, H. W. (2008) The felt sense of natural environments. *The Folio* 21(1), 63–72.

Schwartz-Salant, N. (1998) *The Mystery of Human Relationship: Alchemy and the Transformation of the Self.* London: Routledge.

Shepard, N. (1996) *The Living Mountain: A Celebration of the Cairngorm Mountains of Scotland.* Edinburgh: Canongate Classics.

Siddons-Heginworth, I. (2009) *Environmental Arts Therapy and the Tree of Life.* Exeter: Spirits Rest.

Swanson, J. (2001) *Communing with Nature: A Guidebook for Enhancing Your Relationship with the Living Earth.* Corvallis, OR: Illahee Press.

Ulrich, R. (1984) View through a window may influence recovery from surgery. *Science* 224, 420–421.

Van Gennep, A. (1960) *The Rites of Passage.* Chicago: University of Chicago Press.
Williams, M., Teasdale, J., Segal, Z. and Kabat-Zinn, J. (2007) *The Mindful Way through Depression: Freeing Yourself from Chronic Unhappiness.* New York: Guilford Press.

Chapter 5

Practice issues in moving counselling and psychotherapy outdoors

In reality therapeutic practice and process within counselling and psychotherapy are interdependent and not always distinct; both feed into and fold back on one another, and in one sense practice becomes therapeutic process and therapeutic process becomes essential to practice. Indeed, there are those in the field who have argued that practice itself is central to the evidence base of counselling and psychotherapy (Barkham and Mellor-Clarke 2003). In this chapter I want to explore certain practice issues that come to the fore when taking therapy into outdoor spaces. First I will look at the concept of the frame in counselling and psycho-therapy. I see this as something which makes the process of therapy unique and different from other forms of therapy such as occupational therapy. The counselling relationship places confidentiality and safety as central to the development of a therapeutic relationship. The four walls of the therapy room act as a safe container and can be seen as the solid geographical frame of the work; the door can be shut, disturbances such as noise are kept to a minimum, and others would not enter the room when a session is in progress. Things such as temperature and physical comfort are also seen as important, and unless the weather was very severe or perhaps caused travel disruption, it would not tend to impact on a session. When taking therapeutic work outdoors all of these things impinge upon the process and have to be thought about. The therapeutic relationship is also affected and challenged in a number of interesting ways when moving outside, and I will explore what can happen in this process and ways in which this can be worked with.

Based on a number of years working in peer supervision, Hayley Marshall and I wrote an article on how the frame is reconstructed in outdoor therapy and also how being outdoors can have an effect on the therapeutic relationship (Jordan and Marshall 2010). I will make reference to some of the article here and build upon and expand it, in order to more fully elaborate some of the practice issues in moving outdoors. What I have found is that the therapeutic relationship and the therapeutic process become more multidimensional when moving outdoors and operate on a number of different levels simultaneously. What also happens is that everything becomes a more fluid and unfolding relational process. This seems to mirror nature itself which is defined as a vital, relational, unfolding dynamic process. So indoors what may be a 'static' agreement, mirroring the containment and confidentiality offered by the room space, becomes more of an evolving and negotiated process when moving outdoors. For example when you cannot guarantee confidentiality because of bumping into somebody when walking and talking, confidentiality becomes more fluid and works on a number of different levels in different ways. As we have looked at in understanding therapeutic processes outdoors, things become more of a moment-to-moment process, moving along to moments of meeting. First I will look at the history and background of the therapeutic frame and why it is central to understanding different aspects of safe, professional and ethical practice.

Frame-based counselling and psychotherapy

In the early days of psychotherapy as Freud and his compatriots were working out ways in which the talking cure could be conducted, it would not be unusual for Freud to analyse his patients walking through the streets around his home in Vienna. As psychoanalysis developed, the concept of the frame evolved to contain the transference feelings evoked in the therapeutic relationship between therapist and patient (Gabbard 1995). The therapeutic frame and being in an indoor space (more often than not the therapist's room with two chairs or a couch) became synonymous with one another. In order to hold clear boundaries, psychotherapy needed to be conducted in an indoor space, where issues such as role, time, place and space, clothing, language, self-disclosure and related matters such as physical contact could all be controlled, normally in the service of preventing transgressions such as sexual intimacy from occurring between therapist and patient (Gutheil and Gabbard 1993). However recent developments in psychology (Holmes 2010), psychotherapy (Maxfield and Segal 2008; Madison 2004) and ecotherapy (Jordan 2009) have all sought to advocate and practise therapy in non-traditional settings such as clients' homes, in the community, institutional contexts and in natural settings. Luca (2004) says that maintaining the frame in psychotherapy is the result of trial and error, as well as modifications which sometimes go unnoticed in the course of psychotherapy. What Luca suggests is that even where a clear contract might be set by therapist and client at the beginning of therapy, this does not mean it cannot be open to flux and change. This then sets the scene, first for a discussion of advocates of 'frame therapy' (Madison 2004), such as the communicative school of psychotherapy.

The 'frame' of practice identifies counselling and psychotherapy as being a unique practice of therapy in contrast with 'occupational therapy', 'retail therapy' or 'sports therapy', as the word therapy can be applied to lots of different activities in lots of different contexts. What makes counselling and psychotherapy unique is the concept of boundaries and the frame (I will use these terms interchangeably to signify the unique aspects of the practice of counselling and psychotherapy). The frame of psychotherapy feeds both into the practice and into the identity of the practice and therefore the idea of counselling and psychotherapy as a professional practice and the identity of the psychotherapist as a competent professional.

The frame of psychotherapy relates to the professional and ethical conduct of the psychotherapist, and contributes to the safety of the endeavour for both therapist and client. Langs (1979, 1982), writing about the contractual issues in psychotherapy, states that all people universally require, albeit unconsciously, stable ground rules. This links into the idea that providing a relationship that is unambiguous, consistent and reliable may be considered as a strong facet of the healing force of psychotherapy. The communicative school of psychotherapy that Langs founded places the idea of the therapeutic frame as central to aspects of why and how therapy becomes therapeutic for both client and therapist. However, from a communicative perspective the boundary conditions of the therapeutic setting offer both parties a dilemma. On the one hand, there is a safe containing stable space; however this is counterbalanced by a deep existential sense of the limiting and restricting nature of the therapeutic environment, which mimics the finiteness and vulnerability of life itself (Holmes 1998). In this way the frame of therapy is said to be holding for both parties but also has the potential to be immensely anxiety-provoking. The communicative school argues that the frame is central to the therapeutic process in psychotherapy and forms the main focus for emotions expressed both consciously and unconsciously in relation to it.

Langs (1982) sees the frame as providing the ground rules that define the space and the manner in which the therapy is conducted. Langs states that psychotherapy should be carried out in a soundproof consulting room in a private office in a professional building. He goes on to say that there must be set positions for therapist and client, total confidentiality, a one-to-one relationship and absence of physical contact. Langs refers to the 'deviant' frame whereby the therapist fails to set up the ground rules and context of therapy work; the deviant frame results in absence of the proper conditions for any psychotherapeutic work to take place.

By focusing on the frame as the definition of psychotherapy I am focusing on an aspect of the therapeutic 'environment' within which psychotherapy commonly takes place (Milton 1993). However this presents some interesting issues, in that the frame is a shared construction between client and psychotherapist. If tied into an indoor space, as Langs suggests, what happens in relation to the frame in an outdoor environment if it is dependent on the setting of a private room? My research and practice in outdoor natural spaces challenges the notion of the frame as 'held' within an indoor environment. By conducting psychotherapy outside the traditional confines of an office, it can be seen by other psychotherapists and professionals as a 'transgression' of the traditional boundaries of therapy. Zur (2001), in discussing out-of-office contact with clients, states that interacting with clients out of the office has traditionally been placed under the broad umbrella of dual relationships. A dual relationship in psychotherapy occurs when the therapist, in addition to his or her therapeutic role, is in another relationship with his or her client. However Zur argues that stepping outside the office can be very therapeutic for clients as long as it is part of an articulated and thought-out treatment plan. Bridges (1999) proposes that in talking about the meaning and construction of the boundaries they become the therapeutic vehicle for deepening the therapeutic work and relationship. In challenging the idea of the frame as held statically, Hermansson (1997) proposes that boundary management is a dynamic process where the therapist is continually applying professional judgement in the complex terrain of human relationships and emotions.

The holding of clear and consistent boundaries in counselling and psychotherapy is also linked to the professional integrity of the therapist. As therapists are dealing with difficult and sensitive emotions, the fiduciary nature of the contract between the parties affords that the therapist acts in ways that protect the vulnerability of the client and do not lead to abuses of power and trust (Haug 1999). This issue of professionalism is very important, as is the investment I have in maintaining the professional identity and focus of any counselling and psychotherapy work that is taken outside. I am also aware of how this work is seen by other counsellors and psychotherapists and I feel it is important for it to be seen to be conducted in a safe, professional and ethical manner.

The centrality of the idea of a 'frame' as indicative of safe, professional practice links to the idea that the frame is synonymous with the room. Paradoxically the room is not the frame, but merely a geographical container of the work: the frame is a metaphor, something that is created by the therapist through contracts and boundaries and that the client is then invited to participate in. The frame in this sense is a spatial metaphor that the therapy operates through. Containing the therapeutic work outdoors is very important because therapist and client are now in a much more dynamic and unfolding environment, rather than a static room space, and this can be done in a number of ways.

I will now begin to look at some of the practice issues in setting up a therapeutic frame outdoors and offer examples of how to manage some of the situations that may arise to challenge both therapist and client when moving outdoors.

Assessing clients

One of the central questions for taking therapy into nature is: what sorts of clients may benefit from this experience and how might I assess them as suitable for working outdoors? One of the tensions in taking the work outside of a room environment is whether both therapist and client are moving away from something difficult in the work or whether, by moving outside, there is an opportunity to deepen and explore different aspects of the therapeutic work together.

It is certainly the case for some clients who experience a lot of interpersonal difficulty and find human-to-human contact difficult that moving into a natural space may mediate the human-to-human aspects of the process, allowing the client to feel safe and comfortable enough to begin to make contact with the therapist. This may be true with clients experiencing more severe and enduring mental health problems, but could also be true for certain client populations seen by therapists in private practice. There are some key similarities with assessing clients for counselling work generally and some unique features of assessing people for outdoor work. One of the key challenges in working with clients and taking them outside is how they have initially presented for therapy. The majority of clients I now see outdoors have referred themselves specifically because they want to work outdoors in nature or have a strong interest in doing so at some stage in the therapeutic work. There are other challenges when the work has originally started in an indoor context and the therapist feels the client would benefit from working outdoors, as part of the therapeutic process that is emerging through the work. I will explore both of these aspects of assessment and rationale for working outside. In order to illustrate an assessment for nature-based work I will use a case example, highlighting how a decision was jointly arrived at in beginning to work in a natural context. The first step in an assessment is to get an idea of what the 'presenting problem' is from the client's perspective.

Case example

Sally was a thirty-eight-year-old woman who had a partner and a two-and-a-half-year-old daughter. Sally was a sculptor and was currently working with special needs children at a secondary school. She had referred herself for private one-to-one therapy because she felt cut off and depressed. The birth of her daughter had been traumatic and she had been hoping for a 'natural birth' but had had to have emergency medical intervention. She had experienced difficulties bonding with her daughter. At times during the assessment she became quite tearful.

It is then also normal to take a history in terms of family relationships and previous experiences of therapy, etc. One unique aspect of doing this for someone coming to work in nature is to take some history of their relationship with the natural world and why this is important for them. One of the things that I am interested in is how much of a resource nature is currently for the client and what role it has played historically in terms of their emotional well-being.

Sally talked about her relationship with her mother and father who had separated when she was in her early teens; as part of her schooling she had attended a school where creativity and self-expression were valued and the natural world and the seasons were an integral part of the school curriculum. She had a close relationship with her mother and was more distant with her father. Nature had played an important role in her educational upbringing and was also central to aspects of her art work. She was very aware of colours and visual material in nature, such as textures etc. She was also emotionally affected by the current environmental situation and the plight of certain species; her creative work focused on the natural world and some of these issues. She had also undertaken lots of camping and bushcraft activities prior to her current relationship and the birth of her daughter. At the time of the assessment she wasn't going out at all into nature and stated she had little time set aside for this. I noticed during the assessment (which was in late summer) that she slipped her shoes off and was massaging her feet into the earth; this felt to me an important embodied way of making contact with nature. I commented on this during the assessment and she concurred it was important for her to begin to 'make contact' again in all forms.

Another important part of the assessment is the capacity a person has to make and maintain contact with another. An aspect of this is an awareness of one's own and other people's mental states and one's ability to reflect upon this and empathise with other people.

Sally's presenting problem of feeling cut off and finding it difficult to connect would highlight for us the capacity she has for making contact with another person and her awareness of how her feelings of loss of contact were affecting both her and others, namely her daughter. The importance she felt of making contact again to others and nature felt to me a demonstration of her capacity to connect and be aware of others, but at the same time (as she was presenting herself for therapy) the struggle she was having of feeling connected. The depression she was experiencing seemed to me a 'symptom' of an inner conflict around connecting and feeling connected. I felt that because of the importance of the natural world in her history, conducting therapy in nature was positively indicated and that nature could act as a medium through which we could explore feelings of connection and disconnection, to me, to others and nature itself.

During the assessment it is also good to discuss with the client any fears or concerns they have about being outdoors, such as confidentiality, the weather, physical comfort and ability, and what they might do if they meet people or animals. Next I will look at the importance of having a therapy contract that specifically addresses these issues and what the therapist and client will do in certain instances.

Moving from indoor work to outdoor work with clients

I will illustrate the rationale for moving from indoor room-based work to outdoor work with clients through a case example. The rationale for moving outdoors when the therapy has begun indoors tends to be case-specific and linked directly to the unique work that is being carried out with individual clients. However, things you might want to consider are the client's pre-existing relationship to nature and what role this may have played in their life to date, and whether contact with nature could be used as an additional resource in the therapeutic process. For clients who find the intensity of contact within the room environment threatening, the case example we looked at in Chapter 3, and the idea of nature as a transitional object, showed how nature acted as a mediator of intensity in the therapeutic relationship and allowed the client to be able to feel safe enough with the therapist to begin to form a therapeutic relationship. For other clients the greater democracy allowed by nature outside of the controlled space of a therapist's room can also allow them to feel more relaxed in the work.

The following case example illustrates a piece of work that occurred indoors for six months and then moved outdoors into the setting of the willow dome space where I work.

Case example

Carl had come for therapy suffering from the symptoms of post-traumatic stress disorder (PTSD) following a road traffic accident a year previously. We followed a course of treatment recommended for PTSD in order to help Carl deal with the feelings of panic, depersonalisation and depression he was suffering from. We also looked at Carl's experience growing up and how this experience had affected him on an emotional level. This was sensitive work and Carl needed to feel very safe within a contained space, and the safety of the room, which represented a secure base for him, alongside the therapeutic work with me, allowed the symptoms of PTSD he was experiencing to significantly lessen after six months. In the next phase of our work we discussed how Carl could start to resource himself and find ways in which he could regulate his affect and lessen some of the stress he experienced in life in order for the panic attacks he had experienced in the past not to return. Carl had a strong and pre-existing relationship with the natural world and also a long-standing interest in the practice of shamanism and energy healing. Carl knew that I also practised outdoors and was interested in this aspect of my therapeutic work; we discussed this in the sessions and how we could explore the possibility of working in a natural setting. Carl was interested in the use of ritual as well as the healing power of just being in nature and wanted to explore this in the next phase of our therapeutic work. We agreed that as part of developing resources in his life to enable him to feel less stressed we would work in nature for the next three months, looking at creative ways Carl could support himself and regulate his emotions using nature as a co-therapist and space for healing.

The therapeutic contract

This is the most important aspect of setting up the practicalities of working therapeutically in an outdoor natural space. Issues of confidentiality, timing, weather, boundaries and the therapeutic relationship itself are all interlinked and can to some degree be accounted for in the therapeutic contract. The contract is part of the professional practice of the therapist and is linked to their indemnity insurance, the ways in which they have been trained, and the regulating bodies they belong to, such as the British Association for Counselling and Psychotherapy, the United Kingdom Council for Psychotherapy and the Health Care Professions Council. The contract normally states that the therapist will abide by an ethical code, and covers such aspects as confidentiality (the limits to this), payment, session duration and frequency, and what to do in relation to cancelled sessions and holidays. At the time of writing the professional bodies have not published any written material on practising outdoors. In terms of insurance it is worth checking with your insurer with regard to their position on working outdoors. Most will cover you for working in different contexts, as long as appropriate health and safety checks have been made and you are not engaged in risky activities such as climbing or kayaking, etc.

In terms of a contract for counselling and psychotherapy outdoors, this needs to state explicitly certain unique aspects of working outdoors. These can then be discussed in more detail with the client during the assessment process and initial sessions, alongside usual discussions about session length, holidays, costs and cancellations. An outdoor therapy contract might contain unique elements which need to be adapted to the sorts of therapeutic work you are engaged in and the outdoor contexts within which you might practise. These are examples of what you might want to include, but they need to be relevant and appropriate to where and how you are working outdoors:

- In terms of working with environmental issues which may affect us in outside/natural settings we may at times need to negotiate around the weather, terrain and other factors such as noise, temperature and people wandering into our space. All of these may impact upon a session. As far as possible I will try and maintain a safe therapeutic space for you to work in. However in working outdoors it may not always be possible to maintain absolute confidentiality at all times and we can discuss how we will manage our contact with others during a session and what to do when this occurs.
- In terms of health and safety outdoors I assess routes for risks and hazards carefully and will inform you of any risks where necessary. However not all contingencies can be covered, and in working outdoors, you accept that risks may arise for whatever reason and that I have taken all reasonable steps to address these risks and maintain your personal safety.

The fact that the weather impinges on a session may mean that as part of the contract both therapist and client agree to move their work back indoors and define the practicalities of how this will be negotiated, leading up to a session outdoors that may need to be relocated due to the weather conditions. The fact that there may be people walking by when a session is in progress can also be seen as part of the unique aspect of working therapeutically outdoors. This can provide rich material for both therapist and client to work with if it relates to some of the struggles that have brought the client to therapy.

There are those who do not place as much, if any, emphasis on the boundaries in this way and see them as potentially limiting to the therapy. Totton (2010) makes the case for the importance of boundlessness in counselling and psychotherapy practice. Totton argues that we have over-professionalised therapeutic engagement and in this sense have allowed it to become over-restrictive of both the process and an exploration of true feeling. This is not a view I share but none the less it may speak to some who feel they do not want to place so much emphasis on the boundaries in outdoor work.

Beginning sessions and setting up the therapeutic space

One of the initial challenges of losing the room as a physical and metaphorical container for the work is how to begin and end sessions with the client and how to denote therapeutic space in an outdoor context. Beginning and ending the session outdoors is an aspect of the unique way the work is set up in an outdoor space. Without the confines of a room with a door and a waiting space, the therapist is faced with the challenge of how to begin the therapy and how to mark the space where therapy starts and finishes. Without the aid of the room, the clock and the door to denote aspects of this space and the particular sorts of conversations that occur within a counselling context, the therapist has to find ways to begin and mark the therapeutic space. This is a particular challenge when meeting clients in public spaces such as car parks and moving off for a walk. The therapist is faced with questions such as when does the therapy begin? And what denotes this as therapy and different from just a chat whilst walking in the woods? The following example illustrates one aspect of this process.

Case example

A therapist and client met in a car park by some woods. After greeting one another they began to walk down a track; as they started on the track the therapist asked the client to just bring themselves into the space by breathing and slowing down in silence as they walked; the therapist then pointed to two trees further down the track, saying 'when we walk between those two trees we'll begin the session proper'; they then began the session as they passed by. And again on the return the same trees denoted the finish of the session. The client and therapist parted ways in the car park, saying goodbye.

Some therapists may not need to denote the beginning and ending of a session in such a literal way, and are happy to move the session from social talk into more therapeutic talk without the need of such concrete markers. However, for some it may be difficult to make this shift which, as we will see in the following section, impacts on the therapeutic relationship. One of the challenges and opportunities of moving outside is the increase in mutuality between therapist and client; this may happen because the natural space is a shared space rather than the room which is normally under the therapist's control. So it may be that the client needs to feel the shift from what could be just a 'walk in the woods' to something that has a different purpose and focus. Without the geographic space of the therapy room, other markers can be set up to denote different forms of space and therefore different sorts of conversation. Often crossing bridges or choosing a natural object or location to move beyond could denote the beginning of therapy. These geographical markers can act in place of the emotional geography of the therapy room (Bondi and Fewell 2003), as a way of denoting therapeutic space from ordinary outdoor space. Without physical markers, a gentle mindfulness exercise at the beginning of the session may help to move an internal/external process into a different space.

In terms of setting up the therapeutic space, and how this links to the beginning and ending of sessions, the therapist can remain more static and set up in a similar way to the indoor space, but in an outdoor context. When I first moved outside, due to my psychodynamic training it felt very important to me to contain the work, and in so doing for it to feel safe and held, so I chose to work more statically in chairs sitting in a wild garden space. As my confidence has grown in the work over the years, I have worked in different ways, both moving and sitting, and feel comfortable with different ways of working. One way of working outdoors is to set up two chairs (normally camping-type chairs for portability) within a space where you are unlikely to be disturbed, or to use or create a space which allows you to maintain some form of confidentiality. Another advantage of this way of working in nature is that you can normally rig up or use some sheltered space to keep dry if it rains; if cold you may be able to light a fire or have some other form of heat source. I use a willow dome space within a wild managed garden. The willow dome also allows both my client and me to relate to seasonal changes; at different times of the year the willow will be in leaf, sprouting buds, or more skeletal when shedding leaves in the winter. Working from the willow dome allows me to light a fire if need be, and also to place signs up which say 'do not disturb' which allow some form of confidentiality to be maintained (see Figure 5); although this is by no means guaranteed as often people have walked into the space ignoring the signs. Another advantage of working in a wild garden space is that there are various spaces in the garden with different views and different landscapes within which we can sit, and depending on how the client feels they can choose to be in the sunshine or to sit by a pond or to be more in the shade. Next I will look more at issues of confidentiality.

Confidentiality in outdoor settings

Confidentiality is one of the central challenges in working in a setting outside of the room where there is the potential for conversations to be overheard. In this way confidentiality links to the processes between inner and outer experience: how in moving outside we are taking something that is very private into a potentially more public space. One of the ways in which counselling can be seen to work is that very nature of its privacy, that everything is permissible to discuss, and this allows the client to feel safe enough to explore some of the hidden and difficult aspects of their personality and struggles. Knowing that the therapist is keeping this information confidential (of course given the limits around self-harm and harm to others) allows the client to open up more. For some clients it may be important to work on building a strong therapeutic alliance with the client before you decide to make the move outdoors. Ascertaining when to go outdoors and how your client will build a therapeutic relationship to both you and nature is part of the assessment

Figure 5 Breathing space: maintaining confidentiality with signs (Photo: Author)

and will be unique and different for each client. Some sense of your client's attachment patterns will be useful in this (see Chapter 3 for discussion on attachment and nature).

Confidentiality, and understanding how this will be negotiated in an outdoor context, is intrinsically linked to the therapeutic contract that you set up initially with the client. When working more statically, for example sitting on two chairs in an outdoor space, I discuss with clients what I will do if someone enters into the space beyond the signs I have put up. I say I will get up and engage with the person and gently direct them on their way, saying something like 'we are in the middle of something'. The signs I put up say 'workshop in progress' (see Figure 5). A person who has read this will not know exactly what the workshop entails, so the privacy of the client can be maintained. If someone interrupts the session, and if we need to after the event, we can discuss this in the therapy and how the client feels and how it has affected them.

If walking and talking with a client, confidentiality takes on a more fluid aspect. You can agree with a client in the contracting process what you will do if certain circumstances arise. For example, what if you meet somebody when walking? The therapist can take responsibility for this and either go off in a different direction with the client so as to avoid the contact, or if this is unavoidable, a brief greeting might suffice as people pass one another. If you catch up with some other walkers, you may choose to give them a wide berth; if this is not possible, when passing you might decide to stop talking until you are out of earshot, or to lower your voice. Another element might be what to do if you meet somebody either of you knows. Again you can discuss this in advance by exploring how you will manage this; will you engage with them? And if so what will this mean for the session? If it is someone the therapist knows, the therapist might say something like 'I am in the middle of something, we will talk later'. If by some remote chance the therapist passes another client outdoors whilst in a session, then this can be discussed with the client, as it would normally if you make unexpected contact outside of the session. For the client who is participating in the session all things can be brought back into the session and explored if need be, and they can often provide rich material to explore in the therapy.

You cannot account for every potentiality, but the notion that confidentiality becomes a fluid process is a central aspect of this way of working outdoors. It needs to be both thought about in terms of where and how you are working, and made central to your therapeutic contract and discussions with the client. The important thing is to discuss the possibility of what could occur at the beginning of the therapy during the contracting process, as the client needs to be able to give informed consent for what they are signing up to and the potential ramifications of working outdoors.

Case example

A therapist and client were sitting in their usual spot where their sessions took place. This was a spot known to the therapist as in another role she worked as a volunteer conservation worker; she knew the space well, knowing they were unlikely to be disturbed. However on this particular occasion a group of volunteers were working nearby; they came over to check a track and to clear some dead branches; they were then in sight of both therapist and client. The therapist realised she knew some of them and they were likely to come over and say hello. Having contracted for these sorts of possibilities, the therapist discussed moving with the client, but the client decided it was OK to stay. The therapist then got up and briefly said hello to the workers whilst the client sat and waited, in doing this pre-empting any interruptions to the session, and the volunteers moved away to work some-where else. The therapist and client then continued with the session.

Timing of sessions and maintaining boundaries

One of the ways a session can feel boundaried and contained is the time frame that is placed around it. This is normally between fifty and sixty minutes, depending on the therapist. Some therapists do conduct longer sessions, possibly up to two hours; this is to incorporate some experiential work and reflection time into the session. When walking with a client it may not be possible to stick exactly to the time frame; walking a particular route will mean you cannot always account for the speed and pace of your walking, when you might stop, and other factors such as the terrain and the fitness levels of both you and your client. Managing the time without the aid of a clock, which is always present in the counselling room, adds to the challenge of maintaining an exact time. Of course you can wear a wristwatch and check this at regular intervals, but most therapists do not like to do this so overtly. I use my mobile phone which is placed on silent and vibrates ten minutes before the end of the session to warn me we are getting near the end of time, and if we are not heading back from our walk then we need to start doing so. As my client tends to notice me checking the vibrating phone, I let them know that we have about ten minutes left. I also do this when sitting in the willow dome space as again there is no clock and it allows us both to prepare for the end of the session. Sometimes it may be necessary to extend the session by five or ten minutes due to the need to return to the original meeting place and beginning point of the session. All of this can be discussed with the client as part of the process of the session.

Case example

A therapist and client met at their usual meeting place at the beginning of a woodland walk. The weather had caused the terrain to be a little muddy so walking was a bit slower than usual. Both therapist and client tended to walk a particular circular route which lasted approximately one hour, usually arriving where they had started. At about fifty minutes into the walk the therapist's mobile vibrated to let them know they had ten minutes left; they were still about twenty minutes away from their starting point. The therapist let the client know this was the case and they would finish a little later, checking that this was OK with the client.

Another important factor in walking a route with a client is to give the client a choice and autonomy over which route and direction to go in. These sorts of choices and decisions can be very important to the therapy and may link to some of the issues a client may be struggling with, around power or assertiveness for example. However the therapist needs to be mindful in doing this that they still have to maintain some sense of awareness of the time boundaries and how and when they will arrive back at their starting point. In promoting choice, the therapist still has a degree of responsibility for the psychological and physical well-being of their client.

Negotiating around the weather

A question that arises a lot in outdoor work is what to do if it rains or the weather becomes too cold or inhospitable for therapy to be conducted outdoors. In my own practice I have used large umbrellas and tarpaulins in order to protect both myself and my client from the rain whilst sitting outside. I now also have a covered outdoor space I can work in, which is within the wild managed garden space. Other therapists might decide to work outdoors even if it is raining or cold, and discuss this with the client, regularly checking in with them how they are doing and how it feels in terms of their physical and emotional well-being.

Case example

A therapist and client met in their usual spot; it began to rain as they walked. As they walked the therapist checked in with the client in terms of how it was feeling in their body and how this was affecting them emotionally. The client enjoyed walking in the rain and the feel of the wet on their skin; it made them feel more alive and in touch with their body, a central reason why they enjoyed being outdoors.

Having a contract with the client, where discussion takes place around what you will do if it becomes too cold or wet to be outdoors, means that you can decide to move back indoors if need be. This of course may be dependent on the practicalities of the indoor therapy space you use. If you work from home, there may be some flexibility, but if you hire rooms this may need to be thought out in advance. For example, how much notice will you give each other if you decide to move indoors? With the changeability of the climate in Britain where I work, this can present some challenges that need to be thought through and where necessary discussed with the client. In outdoor work the therapeutic contract needs to be seen as a 'process' which is negotiated and transparent, in a sense mirroring the changing dynamic of the natural environment itself, which will impinge upon any therapeutic work in the outdoors. The changing seasons and weather patterns can act as a powerful backdrop to the therapeutic work, or can be used in the foreground by exploring how the ever-changing weather and seasons mirror aspects of life and the challenges and changes that we constantly face.

The frame and the psychological state of the therapist

The way the boundaries of the therapeutic work are understood and held will be different for different therapists and will link to their training modality and the context of their practice. Working in private practice may be different from working in statutory or third sector contexts. Whilst it is important not to let the boundaries get in the way of good therapeutic work, moving outside presents a dual challenge between holding the work in a safe and competent manner, and moving with the work in a dynamic and unfolding way which itself mirrors the unfolding dynamic process of nature. The therapist may want to move outside of the confines of their training and indoor practice as they may feel they want to revitalise their practice. At the same time the move outdoors can provoke a sense of de-skilling, of being unsure how things might work in a much more uncontained space. The therapist may feel they are transgressing the 'rules' of therapy and how they have been trained to practise. These feelings are all quite natural when initially engaging in the practice and process of taking therapeutic work outdoors.

What I have found from my own experience, and in working with other therapists taking their practice outdoors, is that the way the therapeutic frame is held has a lot to do with the psychological state of the therapist. A lot is dependent on how confident the therapist feels in holding the work without the safety of the four walls, which provide a geographical 'frame' and container. An important thing to realise is that the therapist holds an internal psychological frame around the work with the client, in so doing trusting in their own confidence and competence to be able to hold a much more dynamic and fluid process which unfolds in an outdoor context. This frame is also held within the quality of the therapeutic relationship between the therapist and client. Other therapists with whom I have worked have found it easier to work outdoors the more they have engaged in some of the struggles and challenges of working in this way and have felt more confident in doing this. Their competency has grown as they have felt more able to work in an unfolding dynamic environment by holding on to a sense of an internal frame which they carry with them into different contexts and situations. An example of this might be where a client appears to be just 'chatting' to the therapist as they might be when walking with a friend in the woods. The therapist notices this is happening and gently guides the conversation back into the area of emotions and difficulties that brought the client to therapy in the first place. Casement (1992) proposes that containment can then be seen to rest with the skills and competency of the therapist in being able to both hold and contain the work within whatever space they find themselves. A clear initial contract and explicit framing of the experience allows for both client and therapist to be clear about some of the ambiguities of the therapeutic work outdoors.

Identifying potential hazards and managing risk in outdoor contexts

An aspect of working outdoors with clients is to manage the physicality of the process and to hold some responsibility for the physical safety of your client or group. Carrying out risk assessments of where you are going to work is an important part of managing the physical process of working outdoors, and providing an audit trail of how you have thought about some of the potential risks and hazards. This might include what mechanisms you have put in place in order to address these risks. A typical risk assessment will identify any potential hazards or risks, such as terrain, weather, equipment failure (for example if camping or hiking with groups), any medical issues, transport to and from the location, and any behavioural risks that may present themselves in relation to the client group you will be working with. If you are working in statutory settings or other contexts outside of private practice, it may be that the agency you are working with has its own mechanisms for risk assessment and health and safety. This is certainly true of those practising outdoor therapy in the National Health Service in the UK. It is important to demonstrate a clear audit trail of thinking about risks and assessing them, and the mechanisms you have put in place to manage any risks that might occur.

Working in more remote locations with individuals and groups also presents some physical as well as emotional challenges that need to be addressed and managed. Therapists working in more remote or mountainous locations need to be skilled in working with groups in the outdoors, or have a co-worker who possesses these skills. Therapists need to be conversant with reading maps, negotiating difficult terrain and weather, dealing with hazards and emergency procedures, and able to ensure the group has the right equipment. They would need to be engaged in planning routes and assessing risks before any trips take place. The objectives of these sorts of trips need to be both therapeutic and linked to terrain and geography. Some therapists who work outdoors hold a dual identity as both therapist and outdoor professional. These 'dual' identities are very helpful in terms of being able to draw upon both sets of skills and trainings when managing the emotional and physical safety of the group (Langmuir 1984; Mountain Leader Training UK 2004) – for example when incorporating something like rock climbing or kayaking into the therapeutic work and being skilled and competent in this way of working, then alongside this being able to hold and work with the therapeutic process of both individuals and groups.

If you are planning to work in this way, then I would recommend training in some of these areas. I undertook a mountain leader training, which enabled me to feel more confident in terms of map reading, negotiating certain types of terrain and being able to hold a group safely in terms of managing and assessing risks. My counselling and psychotherapy training also allowed me to feel confident with holding the emotional process of both groups and individuals. I would still not take a group on a walking trip on more mountainous terrain unless I had a skilled outdoor professional with me. Working alongside an outdoor professional presents some challenges in terms of the ability of the outdoor professional to understand and work with the emotional process of the group, in that they will inevitably become part of the group and the group process. In working in this way both the therapist and outdoor professional have to work within the limits of their competence and be willing to find ways in which they can work alongside each other with a mutual respect for their different roles and focus and where these meet and interlink. I do not advocate those solely trained in outdoor skills (even if some of this has been about managing and leading a group in the outdoors) working as therapists, if they have not had any form of therapeutic training. This also cuts both ways in terms of therapists recognising the limitations of their skill sets when working with groups in more risky and hazardous terrains, or engaging in activities like kayaking or rock climbing without the proper training. Some therapists carry both of these skill sets and are dual qualified in counselling and as a mountain leader or canoeing leader.

Working in more remote terrains involves extending the therapeutic work beyond the traditional therapy hour and working predominantly with groups over a weekend or longer time period. This process quite often involves being alongside the group: camping, sleeping, eating, going to the toilet, and being in social spaces, for example around a campfire, chatting, or cooking. Issues to do with the therapist's identity, boundaries of the therapeutic work and how to negotiate these different spaces all come up in this way of working. The therapist working in this way needs to feel comfortable in moving in and out of these different spaces, both social and therapeutic, and how to be clear about these different spaces.

Concluding comments

In this chapter I have looked at come central practice issues in conducting counselling and psychotherapy outdoors in a safe, ethical and competent way. I looked at the importance of the therapeutic boundaries in outdoor work and the importance of the psychological capability of the therapist in their ability to hold boundaries appropriately outside of the safety of the room context. In exploring the centrality of the frame I outlined how the frame shifts when moving into an outdoor natural setting. Assessing clients for their appropriateness for outdoor therapy is important and this was explored by giving a case example looking at factors important in suitability of clients for working in nature. I also outlined the adaptions needed to the therapeutic contract and how to set up the pragmatics in an outdoor space, thinking about how to begin and end sessions. This is particularly important where the therapeutic space is more 'public' and potentially much less contained than it would be in a room setting. Confidentiality was then explored as a central issue and concern for outdoor therapy; this needs to be negotiated and discussed in contracting with clients for outdoor work, along with thinking about the impact of the weather on sessions. Finally I looked at the importance of health and safety outdoors and some important factors to consider when assessing risks and maintaining both physical and psychological safety.

References

Barkham, M. and Mellor-Clarke, J. (2003) Bridging evidence-based practice and practice-based evidence: developing a rigorous and relevant knowledge for the psychological therapies. *Clinical Psychology and Psychotherapy* 10(6), 319–327.

Bondi, L. and Fewell, J. (2003) 'Unlocking the cage door': the spatiality of counselling *Social and Cultural Geography* 4(4), 527–547.

Bridges, N. A. (1999) Psychodynamic perspective on therapeutic boundaries: creative clinical possibilities. *Journal of Psychotherapy Research and Practice* 8(4), 292–300.

Casement, P. (1992) *On Learning from the Patient.* Hove: Guilford Press.

Gabbard, G. O. (1995) The early history of boundary violations in psychoanalysis. *Journal of the American Psychoanalytic Association* 43(4), 1115–1136.

Gutheil, T. G. and Gabbard, G. O. (1993) The concept of boundaries in clinical practice: theoretical risk management dimensions. *American Journal of Psychiatry* 150, 188–196.

Haug, I. E. (1999) Boundaries and the use and misuse of power and authority: ethical complexities for clergy psychotherapists. *Journal of Counselling and Development* 77, 411–417.

Hermansson, G. (1997) Boundaries and boundary crossing: the never ending story. *British Journal of Guidance and Counselling* 25(2), 133–146.

Holmes, C. (1998) *There Is No Such Thing as a Therapist: An Introduction to the Therapeutic Process.* London: Karnac.

Holmes, G. (2010) *Psychology in the Real World: Community Based Groupwork.* Ross-on-Wye: PCCS Books.

Jordan, M. (2009) Back to nature. *Therapy Today* 20(3), 26–28.

Jordan, M. and Marshall, H. (2010) Taking therapy outside: deconstructing or reconstructing the therapeutic frame? *European Journal of Psychotherapy and Counselling* 12(4), 345–359.

Langmuir, E. (1984) *Mountain Craft and Leadership.* Manchester: Mountain Leader Training Board.

Langs, R. (1979) *The Therapeutic Environment.* Northvale, NJ: Jason Aronson.

Langs, R. (1982) *Psychotherapy: A Basic Text.* New York: Jason Aronson.

Luca, M. (ed.) (2004) *The Therapeutic Frame in the Clinical Context: Integrative Perspectives.* London: Routledge.

Madison, G. (2004) Hospital philosophy and the frame. In M. Luca (ed.) *The Therapeutic Frame in the Clinical Context: Integrative Perspectives.* London: Routledge.

Maxfield, M. and Segal, D. (2008) Psychotherapy in nontraditional settings: a case of in-home cognitive-behavioural therapy with a depressed older adult. *Clinical Case Studies* 7(2), 154–166.

Milton, M. (1993) The frame in psychotherapy: Langs and Casement compared. *Counselling Psychology Quarterly* 6(2), 143–150.

Mountain Leader Training UK (2004) *Walking Group Leader Handbook.* Conwy: Mountain Leader Training UK.

Totton, N. (2010) Boundaries and boundlessness. *Therapy Today* 21(8), 11–15.

Zur, O. (2001) Out-of-office experience: when crossing office boundaries and engaging in dual relationships are clinically beneficial and ethically sound. *Independent Practitioner* 21(1), 96–100.

Zur, O. (2006) Therapeutic boundaries and dual relationships in rural practice: ethical, clinical and standard of care considerations. *Journal of Rural Community Psychology* 9(1).

Zur, O. (2007) *Boundaries in Psychotherapy: Ethical and Clinical Explorations.* Washington, DC: American Psychological Association.

Chapter 6

Therapists' stories – taking therapy outside

The vignettes and stories that appear in this chapter originate from research I undertook with practising therapists exploring their experience of taking their therapeutic practice outdoors into natural settings. I will explore the stories of therapists who have made the transition to working outdoors and some of the joys and difficulties they have encountered in this process. Different aspects of working outdoors will be discussed through the stories. One of the challenges, for those who have been trained within a modality of therapy solely based in an indoor setting, is around their professional identity as a therapist. For some this was a destabilising process where they felt de-skilled and had to re-learn how to do things in a new setting. They were challenged in how to translate aspects of their own therapeutic relationship with nature to their therapeutic work outdoors. For other therapists I interviewed, the shift was not so problematic; for example those trained within a creative arts therapy approach found the move less difficult; as they were used to working with a medium such as art in their work, the move outdoors enhanced the creative ways in which they worked.

For all of the therapists I interviewed, nature played a central role in the maintenance of their own well-being. In my discussions with therapists they talked about a pre-existing relationship with the natural world which was central to their own emotional and psychological well-being, and which they were attempting to marry with their therapeutic training and experience. Some articulated a deep spiritual connection to the natural world. Others articulated nature as a restorative space, where they could recharge their batteries and cope with the emotional labour of therapeutic work. There is a lot of research and anecdotal evidence that natural environments do provide restorative experiences for a stressed psyche, and this reasoning would seem to support research in environmental psychology pointing towards the importance of environmental factors in helping recovery and psychological well-being (Ulrich 1984; Ulrich and Parsons 1990; Ulrich 2000). What was clear was that therapists were using the natural world as a space to restore and revive, both from the therapeutic work itself, but also as an important part of their history and the way that they coped generally with life's ups and downs. Peter's response echoes the struggle that some participants had in trying to articulate what was therapeutic about the natural world, as something difficult to put into words, but very much felt. Kaplan's thesis that nature is restorative psychologically (Kaplan 1990) seems supported in the rationale that therapists gave for the importance of nature in allowing them to recharge and revive themselves.

Peter: For me personally I do get to kind of recharge my batteries in nature on all sorts of levels, you know I can get quite a good physical workout but I can also feel quite deeply touched by the experience for just being in a wild place, you know I often go out into the wilderness on my own for the experience of solitude in a wild place. There are some times when I am standing alone in a glade and I can feel almost moved to tears by something beautiful about it, but not just by that, there's a deeper feeling, I don't know what that is but that's just something to do with I don't know what it is . . . I don't know er, maybe I could try and put words to it but I don't think that would be adequate.

Maria: And what I find is that after seeing several clients, I go off to the pond immediately – and I find immediately I enter and go over the boundary between the main road and the heath, something begins to lift; it is as if something falls off my shoulders. It is not just the animal/human world actually, it is . . . because it wouldn't work for me if I was going somewhere, even if it was natural but it was ugly . . . it is terribly important to me that I am going to somewhere really beautiful. And so there is something for me about actually coming into the presence of love I would say.

Embodied contact

Maria highlights the importance of embodied experience in this process, that there is something very important about connecting with the natural world beyond the intellectual and psychological.

Maria: There are other things that have a similar kind of effect but this is very particular. So yes the embodied sense that when I come onto the heath I notice immediately I feel like a dog (giggles). Because I can smell and I watch these dogs running around and immediately we get onto the heath they are excited, and they roll on their backs and it is like they grind the smell of the grass into their bodies. And that is how it feels for me too. I just sort of suddenly feel spontaneous again because I felt very fixed, and maybe my ego has got very kind of het up about something very petty. And then suddenly I am there on the heath and it is as if those things start to melt and things become fluid again.

Justine talks about the forms of bodily restoration and vitality she feels through being in contact with nature.

Justine: It is at different levels really I think: it can actually feel – I can actually notice if I pay attention that I am actually physically breathing more fully. But there is the sense also of feeling more relaxed, more at ease. And that is one side of it. There is also the side of perhaps feeling really energised. And for instance I am looking out at the garden as I am talking to you, at the wind blowing, and that kind of energy . . . and perhaps if you were walking along by a very active sea that can then pick up a more energetic pace in myself. So there will be a kind of resonance there.

The connection to nature also went beyond just the restorative element; some therapists were seeking contact with nature to deepen a process of connection inside of themselves and related to the concept of an 'ecological self'. Maria highlights what are for her some of the central concerns that underpin her reasoning, and a concept that is very much of importance to ecopsychology (Roszak 1992) and to deep ecology (Naess 1973), that getting in touch with a relational self, beyond the human-to-human world, is of central importance both to her individually and to the rationale for taking therapy outside.

Developing an ecological self

Maria: It is as if going to the heath and going to the pond, pulls up a different part of me. I would say that it is a way for me to get back in touch with my ecological self. But not just my ecological self – I am thinking of myself, with a capital S with a Jungian terminology. That it pulls me into a larger part of myself; which is where I can access again a more mature wisdom if you like.

Maria talks about the different strands of her outdoor work as an ecopsychologist. A big part of her practice is teaching ecopsychology and this highlights aspects that other therapists talked about in my research. For these therapists the work in the outdoors focuses on developing an ecological self through experiential contact with the natural world. Whilst not strictly being psychotherapy, this was seen as profoundly therapeutic, and part of a wider project linked to applied ecopsychology, in order to help people think about reciprocal relationships with the natural world.

Maria: But in a sense what propelled me into that was – it is no good just sitting in lecture theatres lecturing people about the need to live sustainably. You know, somehow we have got to find ways to help people think in a very different way. So that was my first jump-off point.

Doug also talks about the transformative and spiritual potential of the outdoors and how this links to his rationale for taking therapeutic work outdoors and the ecological concerns and goals that underpin this. He draws strongly from ideas espoused in both ecopsychology (Roszak 1992; Roszak et al. 1995) and deep ecology (Naess 1973) around the development of an ecological self. Doug is aware of the therapeutic process associated with the development of this way of being in the world. In this sense Doug (as with a few of my other participants) is committed to an agenda of transformation and activism. From this perspective the self as an isolated entity is questioned. The development of an ecological self can be facilitated by transformative experiences in wilderness environments (Greenway 1995).

Doug's story conveys perhaps most powerfully the central role that nature and wilderness play in his sense of well-being and how he actively seeks out these spaces in order to facilitate the development of his spiritual self.

Doug: And it was whilst I was travelling I had some really massive experiences in areas of wild land, you know beyond my wildest imagination really. I had always recreated in the UK but finally made it to Canada and America. And I think I got exposed for the first time to, you know, vast areas of land where they were wild. And that had a huge impact on me. I had some experiences there which were deeply transformative, and I think that is the point where being in those places became a deeply spiritual thing for me. And I guess to answer your question, finally (chuckles), is in those places that I feel most real.

For Doug this links to an important psychological aspect of the work which facilitates a move to a less 'ego'-bound sense of self, which also seems to inform the way he understands aspects of his therapeutic work. We see again here how the therapist's model for self-healing is transferred and applied to a model for helping others.

Doug: And there are words like 'original nature' or 'indigenous nature' – there is something . . . I feel it in my body though. It is like, I recognise that even at home, if I go off out into the hills or off out to the sea or whatever, that something drops away physically. Like breathing out or losing an anxiety. And what it feels to me like is it is a very original state. Those environments to me are primordial environments, and everything else other than that requires me to hold some kind of a tension – I guess to maintain an ego or something?

This focus and belief feeds into the therapeutic rationale for Doug's work, which is to shift the sense of self as individual to more of a collective and ecological sense of self. These ideas seem to me to link to Jungian notions of a 'psyche' not solely contained within the individual but also spread out in the world (Sabini 2002). Rather than a contained ego-bound self which some might see as an illusion, the psyche is contained both within individuals and within the environment, positing a more ecological sense of self. Doug articulates a coherent theoretical stance towards this process and why working in what he terms a more 'wilderness' environment facilitates this shift in a sense of self.

Doug: I mean if you think about that classic kind of doughnut paradigm with the individualistic, skin-bound ego sense of self in the middle, and then the social sense of self around it, and then outside of that something else: but if you take away the central sense of self, and replace that – in our western – of course we are forced to be skin-bound ego – things in the wild construct where no one gives a fig what you look like, or behave like – they don't care – there is no one there to care. And that reconnects people to the primordial sense of what it is to be human. It gives that space, in a sense for the longest period in our evolution. So it reconnects people to the individuals as well, and it feels very real. I think it helps people get – getting a whole kind of sense of themselves.

This primordial sense of self is strongly linked to a rationale for developing a more ecological sense of self. Doug articulates a position consistent with his affiliation to ecopsychology (Roszak 1992; Roszak et al. 1995) and deep ecology (Naess 1973). It is argued that the human being needs to be interdependent with their environment for 'healing'. There needs to be a marrying between a psychological and ecological sense of self. Greenway (1995) has espoused this link to experience of wilderness, ecopsychology and therapeutic work with groups and this is the therapeutic focus of the work that Doug is engaged in.

Doug: But the psychological sense of self, it does not match that ecological idea of self, and so I think one of the challenges to the healing process is about getting those two senses of self to marry. And we have grown up with that frame of reference that it is 'me' – and 'the world', this is the whole idea embedded in our psychology. But ecologically, yes there are boundaries, and there are edges, but they are incredibly permeable, and there is a very close network of inter-connection which defines what we are, as organisms. So I think, you know, I think that the core of the work is giving people a direct experience of themselves as part of the ecosystem. And then helping them process that and of course that is usually . . . what we have found is, people feel lost and they feel – I mean if you did this and you didn't really group and there wasn't a process of support and people working therapeutically, it would be a horrible experience.

What Doug highlights here is the therapeutic element of this shift in self, which without some sort of therapeutic support and group holding, might destabilise the person. In this way we can see that there is an important psychotherapeutic element to any transformative work in wilderness environments. The development of an ecological self starts with the individual and their emotional and psychological world. Doug then goes on to discuss some important aspects of the therapeutic process in relation to experiencing this expanded sense of self. He highlights the importance of the group as a container and safe space (Bion 1970). The context – sitting around an open fire – is important to this sense of safety in order for participants to process what feels like a profound experience.

Challenges to the therapist's professional identity

An important part of taking the work outside is the challenge to the therapist's confidence and sense of professional practice. This is more challenging for some therapists than for others, and this appears to be linked to their therapeutic orientation and modality of training. I asked Nigel, how was it for him meeting people in a car park and running a therapy session, what were the challenges? His answer reveals his initial fear, that in doing this he was breaking the rules of therapy.

Nigel: It's a good question because I never really talked about this because I felt like I am breaking all the rules about this whole thing, you know the therapy hour and the relationship between a therapist and the client had been a very formal one, particularly my upbringing with transactional analysis.

Maria articulates the challenges to her identity she faced as a therapist working indoors with clients around a secure frame, and how things shifted when she moved outdoors. She highlights the risks faced by therapists who move outdoors and may be seen as breaking the frame and transgressing the normal rules of therapy.

Maria: And then once I had started doing that, and I had understood – you know that really shook me up. I remember doing that first course with D, and just feeling like . . . I just didn't really know how to work outdoors, because all my boundaries completely shifted, and they were completely challenged. So I felt really like the carpet had almost been taken from beneath my feet. I felt like I had to find a new . . . step onto . . . not totally different ground. But it was like the room . . . well yes . . . the room had fallen away. So I had to trust that there was a different frame here. But it is as if it has sort of challenged me to completely do away with any – I have had to completely rely on everything of mine that is inside me. So that my clothes that I wear don't matter, so that my room doesn't matter, all those sorts of things that you use or you can use to hide behind. So this work has helped me to look again at my professional self, to understand what is helpful and what is not helpful to the work of therapy.

Here we can see how Maria's analytic training impacted on her ability to understand and adapt to working in an outdoor environment. We can get a sense of how destabilising this was for her, and just how much (conveyed in the next section) she was transgressing the rules around professional practice within the professional peer group from which she originates. She illustrates this when she talks about her one-to-one work. She conveys the anxiety and fear of being seen by another analyst from her community, and her fears of retribution if she had been seen transgressing with her client by moving outside of the room space. At the same time she also talks about the ambivalence she perhaps feels, which is shown by the way she takes on her professional community and the authority of their position in relation to the work.

Maria: My phantasy was – 'what if I meet another psychotherapist from my organisation . . . and of course they would know immediately that this was my client that I was working with!' – ha, ha, ha! Someone actually asked me, with thirty other psychotherapists present – 'do you work outdoors with patients?' (chuckles) And I sat there and I just started to laugh and I said – 'well what do I do now?' (laughing) 'Am I allowed to talk about that here?' And then everyone laughed and I just started talking about it. Someone who had supervised me was there and we got into quite an argument actually, because she was quite determined that therapy must stay in the room.

Here we see the fears that Maria and other therapists have expressed about 'breaking the rules' borne out in actual experience with peers. The idea that the room represents the containment of the work, and that this is the only safe way to conduct counselling or psychotherapy, is very powerful in the profession, and we can see from Maria's experience just how much she and others are going outside of established norms.

Shifting towards multidimensionality in therapeutic practice

One of the shifts that happen in moving outdoors is a shift to a more multidimensional way of working beyond the way in which the therapist might have been trained. What this gives rise to is a more emergent multidimensional identity for the therapist who seeks to practise outside. Not only does the therapist have to monitor and engage with another within an ever changing and shifting natural context, they also have to listen to the client's narrative and at the same time keep one eye on the weather, the route, and an awareness of the possibility of interruption from another person or noise invading the therapeutic space. Alongside the emotional safety of their client or group, they have to think about issues of physical safety and terrain. Holding a therapeutic frame for the work within this environment requires the therapist to work in a more multidimensional way than they would be required to in an indoor context. Therapists working with a group over an extended period of time, possibly in a more remote location, are required to eat and sleep alongside the group with whom they are working therapeutically. They have to negotiate the different spaces that the group operates within as well as having to hold the space for therapeutic work which is both emotionally and physically safe; all of this makes for a more multi-skilled and multifaceted identity as a therapist.

Maria: And we had this weekend residential recently: and four of us were facilitating and my piece was to actually take people at the crack of dawn down to the sea. And it was the first time that I had done this with a group without D. And it was really interesting for me to see. You know I thought – 'oh I am an old hand at this now' 'this is terribly easy!' I found it . . . I felt really wobbly. I was really surprised. Because I do rely on him to really hold safety issues outdoors. He is Mr Outdoor Man. And we talk about it quite a lot. He relies on me to hold, in a sense, the human relationship safely. I mean of course he does an awful lot in terms of working with the group, it is not that I just do that, but I think that we came into the work together with those different expertise, those different areas of knowledge. So the times that I notice it most are on our solo day, and not everyone has come back and it is pitch black and we are in K.D. and we look at each other. And the group is in silence and we are really anxious about these last one or two people. Will this be the first time that someone actually doesn't return, you know? And it is wild and the rocks are slippery, and dusk was an hour ago. And it is those moments that I think that I wouldn't have a clue!

Maria also highlights how these skills arise in the moment and become clearer on reflection, which highlights just how much the therapists are developing tactical knowledge and practice in the process of engaging in the work and also by reflecting upon it with me in the interviews.

Maria: So, and we did do this once recently. The group became incredibly inquisitive and asking us in really fine detail about how we do this and how we work together. And they were sort of forcing out of us all sorts of things that we didn't even . . . hadn't articulated ourselves, about what we kind of unconsciously do. Really it is so interesting isn't it? And how of course, you and I and him and various other people are very experienced and we do all sorts of things without realising quite what we are doing.

This highlights an important issue for the development of outdoor therapeutic work. In asking therapists to reflect on the process we are identifying previously unarticulated knowledge about practice. This section highlights and reinforces the need for therapists to understand more fully the multifaceted nature of the work outdoors, and to share best practice around issues of safety, both physical and psychological, in working with groups and facilitating therapeutic work in outdoor natural spaces. An important consideration for working outdoors is finding support for the work you are doing in the form of supervision from an understanding supervisor, or perhaps from peers who are interested or actively working in this way.

Maria: Well I mean, in a way, I have touched on this sense that the room is the frame. Very, very clearly that it is wrong to go outside of the room. So that has been very anti . . . that hasn't helped me on this journey. I have had to break rules and completely go out on a limb. And until relatively recently –

in secret as well which doesn't help either. There haven't been that many people who I could talk this through with or try and understand what is going on, because none of my supervisors would understand what I am trying to do. So yes, there have been precious few people that I could call on to help me think about it. Well I think the culture is changing very fast. So that I found gradually – well one of the things that helped me enormously was making my connection with J.B. So that has been a good example of finding someone who is a mentor, and who thinks – has a very similar conceptual framework to me. He is . . . I regard him very much as my senior: and someone who would really understand what I am trying to do, and wouldn't disapprove of taking people outdoors.

Nick also discusses this and the difficulty of finding support.

Nick: And funnily enough my trainer/supervisor didn't buy it at all, didn't think it was going to . . . It was just fanciful really; it was very odd really, he was very, very abrupt with me when I voiced my desire to take my work outdoors!

Martin: What did he say then, what was his kind of position then?

Nick: Just that therapy has . . . that psychotherapy can only occur within the four walls, very much around the issues of confidentiality and holding a safe space et cetera and really because I am new into the field and I am not an academic speaker, I am not, you know, it's one of my perceived limitations I guess but I wasn't really able to voice my case. Do you know what I mean?

The challenge of containment

There are important considerations in taking more vulnerable and disturbed clients outdoors, even though those clients may benefit from being outdoors. The concept of containment in psychotherapeutic work is linked to the writings of Bion (1970) and is further elaborated by Casement (1992). Casement refers to containment as the way in which the therapist holds the difficult feelings of the client in therapy; it is seen as crucial in allowing the client to explore the intense and difficult feelings they bring to therapy. For Casement this is done via the mechanisms of interpretation, reflection and the holding and empathic presence of the therapist. Although Casement does not explicitly mention the room in this process, it is very strongly implied that therapy should be carried out in a confidential room space, such as the analyst's room. However if we examine the process of containment, it is largely down to the therapeutic skills of the therapist and their ability to hold the client. Geographical spaces may very well be important in this process, but for therapies conducted in outdoor natural spaces, the geographical space does not necessarily have to be the room. Maria highlights this issue of how to contain the work, and what feels important to her about the safety of the outdoor space she works within, in particular how to hold people who may be very distressed.

Maria: And I suppose one of my questions is for example – one of my patients who's completely core . . . all the work is in the transference. It is not a way that I normally work, but she is so borderline and . . . quite often going into what I would call a psychotic area. And she is one of the people who has asked me to work outdoors with her. Now it may just be that it would transform something: but I have never felt . . . that is one person that I would absolutely have to have a proper set-up outdoor working space.

Martin: Yes, for it to be contained in a way.

Maria: There is something about containment that is terribly important. Which I think is what my ex-supervisor was banging on about really. So it is interesting to think about what does make a space properly contained, for very deep work.

Taking therapy outside – journeys into nature-based therapy

This section explores two therapists' stories as they recount their journey into working outdoors. They discuss the rationale for taking their work outdoors, the challenges of this and the unique ways in which they have understood the natural context as important to the therapeutic process.

Delia's story

Delia's account, which follows, reveals what she brings to the work in terms of her identity as a psychotherapist, trained within an arts-based modality, and the evolution of this identity from nursing and holistic practices like shiatsu. Delia points out the benefits of her psychotherapist identity, in that it enables her to hold the emotional work with her dying clients at depth, but at the same time she points out the limitations of psychotherapy and the importance of empowering clients. This links to a central point she makes about resources both for herself and for her clients and colleagues; she sees nature as a resource for the work and I found her pragmatic spirituality refreshing.

Importance of a 'psychotherapist' identity

Delia starts by discussing the different parts of her professional identity that she brings together in the work and that form part of her multifaceted skills base; in this sense the holism she brings reflects the focus of what she does. However she makes an important point, seeing her psychotherapist identity and skills as central to the ability to hold the emotions provoked by working therapeutically outdoors; she sees her training as a psychotherapist as central to this ability.

Delia: And so when I am working with patients, people from the hospice, patients from the hospice or . . . they are not actually from the hospice, but they are people who are terminally ill but they may not be from the hospice. I bring all three of those to the work but the main one I think, in holding the therapeutic boundary, would be the psychotherapy. What the people talk about, I tap into my nursing because I have worked in the hospice. But the actual containment of it, and my training as a group facilitator which was during my psychotherapy training, those are definitely the things that I feel are important.

At the same time as seeing the importance of her psychotherapy training in enabling her work, Delia can also see its limitations, and the potential a helping relationship may have to disempower people's abilities to find resources in order to heal themselves outside of therapy.

Delia: It is the therapeutic relationship. And the other things that make a therapy effective seem to be things outside that. Like the social context and the 'hope for change' and all these things. And I think that therapy then shouldn't be so 'up its arse!' (laughs) In that when I have got clients, groups or one to one, I want them to be able to resource everything that is available. And that will include their own ability to resource poetry, to resource nature, to resource how therapeutic it is for them to go for a walk.

Delia discusses the importance of healing space and holding space, a container for the work to evolve within. She feels that her psychotherapy training has been important in allowing her to do this, and at the same time she highlights the central importance of creating a form of sacred space in order for the work to take place. In discussing her background and influences she makes an interesting reference to the concept of the Asklepian healing temples, utilised in Ancient Greece as spaces for holistic healing. They were often situated in beautiful spots and focused on both bodily and psychic healing, with particular emphasis given to the healing potential of dreams (Kearney 2009). What Delia does (as do other participants) is point towards the importance of the multifaceted nature of healing within the therapy process; that in taking therapy outside of a purely verbal room-based process we open up the space for a more multidimensional understanding of healing from psychological distress. In this sense we see how therapeutic effect is contextual, shaped and immanent to a holding space, and that the natural space where therapy takes place is an important part of this. Delia elaborates upon this.

Delia: I think it is holding the emotional dialogue: we do take care to create the space and I think that is one of the things that I have always found really important. But I think that comes as well from palliative care. Because I was really influenced by Michael Kearney and his work who talked about the Asklepian Healing Temples, and it was like the environment and there was this wonderful phrase that he quoted, 'The most we can do is to prepare and hold the space for where miracles can happen'.

In relation to this healing space, Delia talks about the importance of her training as a psychotherapist and how this has enabled her to both create and hold a different kind of emotional space where the therapeutic work can take place.

Delia: And it reminded me of the chemical chamber where all this transformation takes place, so I would be really aware as I have been training as a psychotherapist, to create that space through the actual environment. Literally that it is a contained environment with no interruptions or as few interruptions as possible, but also something about me, and how I can bring a holding presence. And I would do that I think by my own sort of self-knowledge and my own therapy – big time my own therapy. And then the idea of the professional ethics and the sort of codes of conduct that are sort of behind the shoulders guiding it.

In terms of the environment where the work takes place, Delia makes the point that the cycles of the seasons seem very important in the work, in particular with dying patients, and how the seasons and the living processes of nature are an important reflection on the cycles of life and death. As Delia says, the living process of nature acts as a very powerful mirror, a kind of 'coming home'.

Delia: I think partly it feels, people have described it, including the facilitators, as a coming home. And I don't think it is literally the yurt, I think it is . . . there is a sense of coming home in nature. And so I will talk about that in a minute. But the yurt particularly I think is also . . . because it is a seasonal thing . . . it is like they have made it another year and they have come back and it is spring again and that . . .

Martin: [I am referring to the yurt which is situated where we are talking, being put up and taken down each season] So it goes up seasonally and it comes down.

Delia: Yes so it is a real mark of things, that they have survived another year. And then the fact that we are sitting in a circle, within a circular building within a circular area of grass within the trees, it feels to me – and they talk about feeling really safe – and what I notice is that very quickly (whereas in the cottage and maybe a bit in the hut there is a lot of talking as if it is a bit of a coffee morning to begin with) they drop into quite deep feeling quite quickly, which can be negative feelings but it can also be quite sort of soulful and positive.

Delia refers to the relationship between space and affect, how certain spaces and places have the capacity to either inhibit or facilitate the expression of emotions. In particular Delia relates this to the space of the hospice where the day care of patients is carried out; that this is not always a safe space conducive to therapeutic work. She contrasts this with the natural spaces she works in, and these have the capacity to take people to more of an emotional depth. This is important for understanding the nature of the frame in an outdoor setting and at times its relationship to geographical holding space.

Delia: Well, if you are thinking about therapeutic space, in the place that I am talking about it is quite difficult to contain the space. Partly that is because day care is itself set up with kind of big doors coming into the office. So people might go past even if you say please don't, they do, and the phone rings. It is really disruptive, so after a while I knew that you couldn't actually take people into that depth there because they may be interrupted.

We continue this conversation about the relationship between space and affect, Delia seeing circles and the fire as important for part of the process of moving into emotional depth.

Delia: Well we would [work in depth] around the fire. Because I think that is far away enough from people, and where people shouldn't come in. But this doesn't . . . I think I can identify with places in the wood that feel holding and places that don't.

I am intrigued by this point and ask her to explain more. She then makes reference to the context of where we are sitting, which is in the woods but at a bench near to the main house and where cars park for the workshops. She highlights the sorts of conversations that might happen in the space where we are sitting.

Delia: So this doesn't, it is quite nice but this is more of a sort of – 'Hi, how are you?' – beginning point, it is not a depth point.

We then talk about the different spaces in the woods and how they relate to the possibilities for therapeutic work.

Delia: Yes, I think it would be a feeling; it wouldn't just be like observing it. I would have to feel that it feels alright. And this place here feels nice but open – so not containing. Not dangerous, so there might be degrees of . . . you know it feels fine but it is not a containing place. The yurt absolutely feels containing, I think because it is closed and even if you hear people outside you are inside. The only time that the boundary was ever threatened was when somebody (who I think knew R. or something) came and sat on the grass and didn't realise we were inside. We could hear them talking so I had to move them. So I would maintain the boundary by doing that, and ask them to leave. There is also the little labyrinth up there, where we have been, and we have sometimes sat round there and certainly there are pathways even that feel containing. That pathway along there, even though sometimes people who shouldn't (well not shouldn't), public people, walk it. There is a sort of ritual, where we have walked from here or from the yurt, to the labyrinth and a lot of talk happens there.

Delia as an arts therapist sees nature as a resource for the therapeutic work she is engaged in. In this, she takes a different view from some who, in viewing nature as a sacred space, would have a critical view of a therapist 'using' nature in this way, seeing it as a reflection of the dominant paradigm of industrial society exploiting natural resources. Although I see the validity of this position, in protecting nature from exploitation and harm, I do not see in this case that the natural world is being exploited.

Delia: Yes, I mean the word resource comes back to me all the time. I don't think of nature as the be-all-and-end-all, I just really value it as a resource. And I am not really in my sort of ecological stuff, I am much more interested in how to use it in a positive way, rather than how to make the world greener. I know that is part of it, that if we can . . . but I am much more on that kind of . . .

Delia and I discuss this point further as I think it is important in how 'nature' is positioned in the therapy; we talk about the impossibility of not 'using' nature and the interdependency of things. This does not mean everything is beautiful, but that there is death and decay also in this interdependency.

Delia: And it is a resource that heals. It is not a resource that I am going to use just for myself. It is being . . . you know all animals use nature don't they, well culture is . . . all the indigenous cultures . . . all flowers use nature, everybody . . .

Martin: There is an interdependency?

Delia: There is an interdependency, yes that is the word. It is interdependent, that is true. I think that therapy, I get annoyed when people try to narrow down therapy, and I think that also I get annoyed when people think that therapy is the only bloody thing in the world! Because when you look at the research the actual method of therapy is really almost irrelevant. So it is not this really, really small thing, therapy. I think that you have to have the therapeutic training and your own therapy in order to do it. But then it is to say to people, look what resources you have got. So when they leave your room they can still meditate under a tree or go and sit by the sea and listen to the waves. And they can look at pictures and learn the myths.

Delia is offering another critique of psychotherapy and the possibility of disempowering people in the process. She refers to the multifaceted nature of healing from distress and just how important it is for clients to begin to feel empowered in this process.

One of the central aspects of the use of nature for Delia, in her work as an arts therapist working with dying people, is the way that nature as a process, moving in seasonal variations, mirrors aspects of life and death and can be understood in this way for those facing end of life issues. She starts her work with groups by getting them to build a mandala as a creative representation of themselves and their feelings, as placed creatively within a bigger cycle. At the same time the creative act of building the mandala also serves the purpose of taking the group into a different space.

Delia: Like now we always create a mandala at the beginning of the session.
Martin: Why would you say the rituals are important?
Delia: Well partly, it is important to me again as a boundary thing. So very, very simply you are just marking the beginning and the end. So we create something together to mark the beginning of this special time, and then you undo it to mark the end of it. So it acts as a gateway that you open and so on a very simple level it is that. And it also brings the group together, but I think also as in any ritual, it takes people to a different level of consciousness. It is locating, we are here, and marking the cycle of the seasons, so that you have got, you know, that on to it: and the elements. So you become part of this bigger cycle. And so it kind of places you, so that is a sort of grounding exercise. It places you, you create this thing which marks the beginning of the boundary, and then in doing it, it invites you to enter this different place.

This echoes an aspect of how therapeutic processes work in nature and the importance of counselling and psychotherapy being in life, in the form of the seasons of the year. At the same time there is the process of death, and life and death are situated within this living process and reflect the process of the group and the work that Delia is engaged in doing. What she also says, which I think is very interesting, is that nature itself holds aspects of this very difficult process. It is an appropriate place to end the story on death and endings themselves, and nature plays a role in helping to make these transitions.

Delia's story reflects the contradictory nature of a narrative in that she both values her identity as a psychotherapist, seeing it as equipping her to work in particular skilled ways in the outdoors and with her client group, but at the same time she points out and critiques the limitations of psychotherapy. She discusses the problem of overdependence on the therapist, how nature provides a resource for the client outside of therapy, but also how we need to enable clients to find these resources for themselves.

In looking at the rationale for going outside, it seems that the client group that Delia predominantly works with in palliative care, those with terminal illnesses and facing death, have provoked her to think about her therapeutic work in a different way. What comes through strongly in her decision to move outside is the reference she makes to the Asklepian healing temples, and a move beyond the medical model of treatment in palliative care. This includes a commitment towards a more holistic understanding of helping clients negotiate end of life issues. She sees nature as a key resource for this work, a space that reflects the seasons of life and a way of understanding life and death within context.

In terms of the therapeutic frame this seems linked to her identity as a psychotherapist which she brings, beyond her training as a nurse, and in this highlights the skills of the therapist in working in spaces outside of the room, being able to hold a boundary and to work at psychological and emotional depth in these spaces. What she says in a sense is very important, in that working in an institution within an inside space, both the room and the wider institution potentially get in the way. She makes the point that nature invites a more shared space in the therapy, that the boundary between therapist and client becomes less clear, that there is more equality in the therapeutic relationship because of the shared nature of the space. As it is not a room that the therapist controls in some ways, the space is more democratic.

In terms of therapeutic process Delia's story highlights some key themes for working in an outdoor natural space. The first issue is seeing experience mirrored within a process in nature, that the seasons and the cyclical nature of life reflect the process of life and death. Delia also sees the importance of nature as a resource to be used for therapy, a creative space that can be utilised by the therapist in order to facilitate the therapeutic work. Delia also makes some important links between the outdoor natural space and therapeutic effect, describing how particular spaces in the wood facilitate or hinder certain therapeutic processes; how some spaces feel more containing and that this links to the depth of therapeutic process that might be achieved in these spaces.

Lastly there are facets of Delia's identity that are highlighted in the story. She makes the point that the competency of the therapist and their training in counselling or psychotherapy are an important aspect of their ability to both be able to hold and be able to understand the therapeutic work in an outdoor natural context. She sees her training as important and something that differentiates her from other professionals, such as nurses, in the palliative care context and allows her to hold a particular sort of therapeutic boundary. In this she highlights an important difference between psychotherapeutic work in nature and work that might be seen as 'therapeutic'. This distinction is important as nature seems to have a therapeutic effect and therefore could be seen as a backdrop to occupational therapy work, for example. What makes the outdoor work psychotherapeutic is the depth of the work and the skill and training of the therapist who is able to facilitate this unique and particular way of working.

Eliza's story

Eliza's story is driven by her strong commitment to Buddhist psychology and practice and how this underpins her understanding of therapeutic work in outdoor natural spaces. This is then placed alongside both her experience as a client of outdoor experiences, which seems to have been a central driving force in her decision to practise outside, and her experience and growing sense of competence in working with groups outdoors. The interview starts as others have done with me asking Eliza about her therapeutic relationship with the natural world. Her response highlights the area of 'space' and the important effect space has on her psychology. It has an interesting resonance for me as it is something I have been, and certainly was at the time, struggling with, both theoretically and emotionally: how to articulate space as something between subject and object.

Eliza: There is definitely something for me to do with space. Space: physical space. So I find, that when I am doing, and we are talking about the work I have done with a client, but also the work that I am doing working with clients: there is something about being not confined physically in the room and being able actually to use that space to be able to move.

This is an interesting point that illuminates the importance of the body in a spatial environment and how this links to psychological states; for example, the sense that the room may be a containing space which holds the work (Langs 1979; Casement 1992), but at the same time for some clients it may feel enclosed and claustrophobic. It also highlights the effect of the room on some clients' sense of well-being and the contrast of physical space indoors and outdoors, something that Bondi and Fewell (2003) have written about in terms of the spatiality of the counselling room. Eliza also elaborates on the relationship between internal and external space and its importance for the therapeutic work, in that an external environment may act to free up internal space.

Eliza: Yes, something to do with, there is an actual physical space that you are in, that you can move around in, and that for me there is something about that, that gives me a kind of . . . suggests a mental psychological space to move around in as well.
Martin: That allows . . . like the exterior space, in a way, mimics or reflects your interior space, or gives you some sense of inner space?
Eliza: Yes and the main thing for me is to be able to move through space, is to free up my . . . my internal process. So particularly if I have got something that I am struggling with, and that I find it hard to work through, or even sometimes to know what I am feeling: to be outside and to move seems to free that up. And that is, for me, that is something that I have done ever since I was a child. So it was a very long lasting . . . it is quite an entrenched thing really. Does that make sense?

Eliza is articulating the importance of an outdoor space and how this relates to an internal psychological space. This then feeds back into an internal sense of being stuck and allows her to be able to free up her inner world, something that being inside somehow inhibits for her. She elaborates further, stating she is thinking aloud, struggling to articulate the process.

Eliza: Yes, and I think, and I am sort of thinking out loud a bit here, but there is also something for me – in that it probably depends on the kind of person you are. Where I can get very stuck with my internal process and I almost like need some feedback from something external. So, I think being outdoors – and this is quite difficult to put into words really – but being outdoors and sort of moving whilst I am outdoors – but it is not just me and my thoughts, there is something external coming. But there is something about the theory of the way that I work as well, and that is something to do with connecting with something that is not me. It is a bit hard to explain.

In the next part of the interview we discussed this idea and Eliza's struggle to articulate these processes. In this sense we are both trying to understand something as the interview unfolds. I am struck by this need to know, which may be my issue more than Eliza's, as there is something in what she and other interviewees are saying, that may be beyond words. What emerges is Eliza's personal interest in and connection to Buddhism as a practitioner.

Eliza: Yes. It just kind of connects with what I was saying there – one of the – as you are probably aware – one of the big aspects of Buddhist theory is this idea that we don't have a solid enduring self, but that a lot of the time we think and behave as though we do. So connecting: I mean in Buddhism, any sort of connection with something that is separate from yourselves, clearly separate, helps to free that sense up, helps us to see the world more as it really is than filtered through our own concepts. Yes?

Martin: Yes the world is more of a process rather than a fixed set of concepts. And yourself as a fixed concept within that; but it is more like the world is a much more fluid process.

Eliza: And also in Buddhism, in really basic sort of Buddhist ideas there is, and there still is, this idea that as well as you have the five senses, the five minimal senses, you also have thoughts that appear in the mind, and our mind is almost seen as a sixth sense. So our thoughts kind of appear, thoughts appear in our mind in the same way as sights appear to our eyes or sounds appear in our ears.

She then goes on to talk about the importance of senses, perception and control.

Eliza: So something . . . and it is very hard for me to put this into words, because a lot of this I am still looking at myself actually Martin. But there is something about being in an environment where more of our senses are engaged, in quite an active way that puts all of those things in perspective and makes it kind of clearer to us. It is a bit like what happens to us in meditation; it makes it clearer to us; our thoughts just arrive in the same way as a vision of the tree that we have just walked past, to us. This connects with what you were saying about it being a process.

Eliza seems to be saying something about issues of process and being in life as having the potential to have a therapeutic effect. She elaborates on this point below, and describes how therapy in the natural world mirrors wider change processes going on for the participating clients. In terms of a therapeutic rationale, Eliza talks about how the group with whom she was working were all experiencing life changes of one sort or another, and how she saw the importance of the natural world as having the capacity to mirror this process as a constantly changing space, a living environment that is always in a process. In some senses perhaps aligning to my earlier questioning, she explains.

Eliza: So part of my thinking around that was that again the natural world, because it is constantly changing anyway, and we react to change, and external change is happening to us: so obviously things are changing everywhere so that seemed kind of appropriate.

Eliza also discusses something of central importance to the rationale for taking therapy outside in her own experience of being a client of outdoor therapy experiences: the sense that an outdoor natural space feels a safer place to encounter more difficult feelings. She articulates this in relation to her experience of being in groups during her counselling training and that some of the negativity of the experience was about being indoors and that an outdoor natural space would make something feel easier.

Eliza: I had very negative experiences of groups and I wasn't happy working in groups at all. And I did have a sense that to do something like that in the outdoors: and this is about what I said about feeling there is more space as well, but I had some sense that it would feel safer to be in a group, if you weren't enclosed inside a room.

However an important point to note is that the outdoors is not necessarily all benign and less threatening. For some people it can be quite challenging, especially in terms of being alone in a natural space. Eliza discusses this, but also highlights its therapeutic potential in relation to the group she is working with outdoors.

Eliza: So there were people who found the outdoor space – I wouldn't say threatening (threatening is probably too strong a word) – because it isn't really that kind of an environment. But they certainly felt uncomfortable at times being in the outdoors, and particularly when they were asked to do things on their own. And that did help a couple of people actually, they stuck to that and actually did things, and they did allow themselves to move away from the group, in a kind of controlled way. So I am thinking of one particular person: it quite altered in a way that she was able to be outdoors. So that was quite a behavioural thing really, and to achieve that she needed to try out in an available space to do that.

As with others I talked to, Eliza experienced some anxiety about starting out and how to work therapeutically outside. Her concerns echo the concerns of other therapists and also illustrate some of the anxieties about physical safety in an outdoor environment. Interestingly, she frames the process as an 'experiment'.

Eliza: It was very much an experiment. I had no idea at all how it was going to pan out; so if anything it was as much a learning experience for me as for my clients. And I did make it clear to them before we started, that it was the first time that I had done any work like this, so I was quite open about that.

She then talks about the practicalities of the process and how she set up the group and where and how the group met. Eliza highlights pertinent issues to do with managing a group outdoors. In particular she discusses aspects of physical containment, the safety of the group, and a clear contract with the group, which is mutually negotiated and agreed in advance.

Eliza: And so what we did: the form of it was that we met for two hours every week for about six weeks. And it is a quite interesting space because it is owned by the council but you get into it via a kind of a park really, you know with a children's play park and things. And then it opens up into a piece of moorland which is quite high up and it has actually got a summit on it really, so if you get to the top you can have a 360-degree view. And it is actually quite wild, but it is contained. And because it is this sort of council-owned space it is contained, so it has got a very clear perimeter.

Martin: And is that important do you think?

Eliza: It felt it, yes, particularly I think last year when I was doing it, because one of the things that my co-facilitator and I were quite concerned about, which in the end wasn't an issue, was people kind of wandering off and getting lost, you know; hurting themselves. Even though it is a very, well it feels like a very safe place for me, physically safe. So we did contract quite clearly with people, that they were to stay within the perimeter of the space, and not just to leave, and not to go away, and if they got very distressed they were to speak to one of us and not just disappear. And it was quite a clear contract in terms of that.

In the interview Eliza talks about how she is just about to run the group again with a different set of clients, and how this second time around her anxiety about these practical issues is much less. This is an important point for the identity of the therapist and the experience of working outdoors over time. It seems with experience by encountering and managing the practicalities of working outside, which she says did not seem as challenging in reality as they did in preparation, she has become much more confident and relaxed about working outdoors.

Eliza: Because I am just thinking about all of this now because we are about to start the group again, and although I think it is important to talk about some of these issues, and the contract: they were much less of an issue in reality than they may have been. So it was a kind of a level of anxiety then, the first time, which isn't there now.

Martin: And why is the anxiety lessened? That is interesting, because they are not such big issues, or because you have done it and it feels like it is a workable process then?

Eliza: Yes. I think it became very clear that we just dealt with most of these issues as we were going around. Because there was one time where we were walking together as a group, and somebody stopped and talked to us. And I had sort of been . . . I hadn't particularly thought through how I would deal with this beforehand: except that I knew that it needed to be managed. And then it did happen and it wasn't an issue. We dealt with – well I dealt with it quite easily – and was polite but didn't encourage the guy to keep talking.

Eliza's story reflects some important identity issues, highlighting particular aspects of her thinking and belief system as a Buddhist psychologist, all of which impacts upon her reasoning and thinking about why she is going outside and how she understands the therapeutic work. If we take her initial rationale for going outside we can see how much this is driven by her experiences of being a client of outdoor therapy. Some of what she experienced in working indoors seemed to have been quite negative for her therapeutically. She wanted to move out of an analytic place inside her head into an outdoor natural space and explore what for her at the time was a personal crisis. This understanding of the outdoors as a changing place feeds into her therapeutic rationale for taking a group outside, as they were also struggling with change issues. The natural world is a constantly changing space and seems an apt backdrop to facilitate this.

In terms of the therapeutic frame, Eliza's story highlights some important concerns for the therapist when making the decision to take a group outdoors in order to work therapeutically. She is concerned about the safety of the group, especially their physical safety. This is managed by talking with the group and setting up a contract which delineates a physical boundary for the work, and also an emotional boundary, for example, what to do if a group member becomes upset.

In terms of therapeutic process Eliza has some very interesting things to say about the relationship between inside and outside space. The space of the outdoors is important, in that it facilitates the exploration of emotional experience in a different way. External space and change processes in nature seem to mirror an internal process: Eliza's Buddhist beliefs influence both how she understands the outdoors and its therapeutic effects. Her ideas link to writing in the field of Buddhism and ecotherapy practice (Brazier 2011). She sees the outdoors as engaging the senses in a different way and that this has an important therapeutic effect. I also liked the idea that we have a fantasy that we can control things like the weather and of course we can't, and that there is something therapeutic in engaging with that.

Lastly Eliza's story says something important about an identity in process as an outdoor therapist. She talks about the excitement of going outside for both herself as a client and for the groups she takes out. What we then get is a strong sense of her increase in confidence after having successfully engaged with a group, and how the next time around, in preparing to work with another group, many of her anxieties have decreased. This is reflected in my own experience of having practised outdoors for four years now: my initial anxieties have lessened in the process of engaging in the work. I have also found this to be true of some other colleagues I have worked with over a period of time: their confidence in the outdoor work has increased as they gain more experience in doing it.

Concluding comments

In this chapter I have reviewed therapists' experiences in taking their therapeutic practice outdoors. A central starting place and an important aspect of the thera-peutic rationale for wanting to work outdoors is the importance of the natural world in the emotional and psychological life of the therapist. Several therapists had a strong and enduring history of going into natural spaces to restore themselves and to find emotional and spiritual solace. Some therapists were driven by a need to take on issues in relation to the current environmental crisis, seeing their therapeutic work as strongly linked to enabling people to develop a more ecological sense of themselves and their relationships. In taking their work outdoors, some therapists experienced anxieties, feeling they were breaking the rules of therapy and being transgressive; others worried about how to contain the work and keep it safe. Some struggled to understand the greater multidimensional nature of working outdoors and how to translate their predominantly indoor-based training into this new setting. Finally I looked at how two therapists had experienced the shift, and the unique perspectives they brought to understanding their work in this new setting.

References

Bion, W. R. (1970) *Attention and Interpretation: A Scientific Approach to Insight in Psycho-analysis and Groups*. London: Tavistock Publications.

Bondi, L. and Fewell, J. (2003) 'Unlocking the cage door': the spatiality of counselling. *Social and Cultural Geography* 4(4), 527–547.

Brazier, C. (2011) *Acorns among the Grass: Adventures in Ecotherapy*. Arlesford: O Books.

Casement, P. (1992) *On Learning from the Patient*. Hove: Guilford Press.

Greenway, R. (1995) The wilderness effect and ecopsychology. In T. Roszak, M. Gomes and A. Kanner (eds) *Ecopsychology: Restoring the Earth, Healing the Mind*. London: Sierra Club.

Kaplan, S. (1990) *The Restorative Environment: Nature and Human Experience*. In D. Relf (ed.), *The Role of Horticulture in Human Well-Being and Social Development: A National Symposium*. Portland, OR: Timber Press.

Kearney, M. (2009) *A Place of Healing: Working with Nature and Soul at the End of Life*. New Orleans: Spring Journal Books.

Langs, R. (1979) *The Therapeutic Environment*. Northvale, NJ: Jason Aronson.

Naess, A. (1973) The shallow and the deep, long range ecology movement. A summary. *Inquiry* 16, 95–100.

Roszak, T. (1992) *The Voice of the Earth*. London: Simon & Schuster.

Roszak, T., Gomes, M. and Kanner, A. (1995) *Ecopsychology: Restoring the Earth, Healing the Mind*. London: Sierra Club.

Sabini, M. (ed.) (2002) *The Earth Has a Soul: C. G. Jung on Nature, Technology and Modern Life*. Berkeley, CA: North Atlantic Books.

Ulrich, R. (1984) View through a window may influence recovery from surgery. *Science* 224, 420–421.

Ulrich, R. (2000) Effects of gardens on health outcomes: theory and research. In C. Marcus and M. Barnes (eds) *Healing Gardens: Therapeutic Benefits and Design Recommendations*. Chichester: Wiley.

Ulrich, R. and Parsons, R. (1990) Influences of passive experiences with plants on individual well-being and health. In D. Relf (ed.) *The Role of Horticulture in Human Well-Being and Social Development: A National Symposium*. Portland, OR: Timber Press.

Chapter 7

Developing your own therapeutic relationship with nature

One of the ways you can develop your nature-based therapy practice is to explore your own relationship with the natural world and use this as a vehicle through which you can understand how you might begin to work therapeutically outdoors with your clients. A starting place to explore your rationale for going outside with clients is to begin with an exploration of their own emotional relationship with nature and how this will translate into your work.

I have personally used nature as a space for healing and as a therapeutic medium through which I can explore and gain support for some of the struggles I am experiencing. I have used nature as a co-therapist, and this was also true of other therapists I talked to, in relation to the sense that sometimes going into nature could be an escape from a painful experience at home. The natural environment became a therapist for the therapist, something they were able to fall back onto both as a holding space for the work and a space for healing.

Ottosson (2007) describes the importance of nature in his own recovery from a traumatic brain injury and the subsequent physiological and psychological problems he encountered. Stating that he moved from simple relationships with inert objects such as stones and rocks, on to more complex relationships with plants and greenery, he was able to utilise nature as a space for recovery from his trauma. Drawing from Searles (1960), Ottosson proposes that the stability and security of the environment was important; due to the crisis, he needed to revert back to simpler forms of relationships. This was followed by graded exposure to more complex sets of relationships via the natural world; this allowed him to find a way back to relating to humans again.

This links to a recent trend in nature-writing literature, telling the story of how the natural world acts as a place that can facilitate healing from a mental health crisis. Richard Mabey's book *Nature Cure* (2008) charts his recovery from depression in relation to the natural world that surrounded him. Tempest-Williams (1991) writes about her process of grief and loss in relation to the natural world surrounding her; place, family and emotion all interweave in a personal journey very much linked to the natural world. These experiences also echo meetings with other therapists working outdoors, where I noticed a lot of informal time was spent by therapists discussing some of their solo therapeutic experiences in the natural world. Therapists discussed the processes they had set up for themselves as a way of exploring the natural world as a therapeutic space for them. It also echoed a lot of my own autobiographic experience of self-directed experiences in nature as a way of understanding myself more deeply as a therapist. Nan Shepard, writing from a literary perspective, evokes her solo wanderings in the Cairngorm mountains of Scotland; nature becomes a place where she finds herself on a deeper and more profound level (Shepard 1996). This also links to recent research on counselling trainees' connection to the natural world as important to their well-being (Hegarty 2010). Wolsko and Hoyt (2012) propose that therapists influenced by ecotherapeutic ideas are often driven by the idea that models of healing for oneself – for example therapists who have had a positive and restorative experience in nature – are more likely to encourage this in their clients. This links to the importance of the experience for the therapist of being a client engaging in outdoor therapy experiences.

For most therapists their own personal therapy is a central component in their training as a therapist. However, in the emerging area of outdoor therapy there is little opportunity for therapists to gain this experience with other qualified therapists, so frequently they have had to set it up for themselves, quite often in the form of a solo trip or journey in a natural location. Some therapists had, however, been able to get experience as a client of outdoor therapy.

If you are unable to participate in an experience with another therapist to begin to explore your own therapeutic relationship with nature, there are some self-directed activities you can engage in. You can start by exploring your own history with nature simply by asking yourself how your relationship with nature has evolved over the years, and how it feels at the moment. This can also be combined with walking exercises and guided explorations within a natural setting, to provoke your emotions and explore how you are feeling about your history and current relationship with nature and how this reflects on your other relationships. Alongside this there are a number of exercises which you can explore in trying to develop and understand your personal relationship with nature.

All of the following exercises should be carried out with an ethic of respect for the land and with the principle of walking lightly upon the earth and leaving no trace. In terms of health and safety it is important to observe certain awareness around the physical and emotional risks of engaging in these exploratory exercises. Always check the weather forecast and wear appropriate clothing and footwear for the terrain and expected weather conditions. Make sure you carry an emergency kit and other items you might need outdoors. Familiarise yourself with the terrain and risks that might be encountered in your chosen natural area. Always tell somebody where you are going and when you anticipate returning.

Exploring participatory processes in nature

As we looked at in Chapter 4 on therapeutic processes in nature, 'participation' as a process explores how we can experience and be present in natural spaces. The process of participation facilitates a movement between an outer and inner experience: if we accept the argument presented by ecopsychology that modern society has a deadening effect on the senses and that this can lead to a wider sense of disconnection and depression, connecting to nature via a sensory engagement is very important for both our mental health and to awaken a sense of vitality and aliveness.

Awakening the senses through participation in nature can be done in a number of ways, and I will outline a series of exercises through which you can engage your sense of sight, touch, taste, smell and hearing.

Sight exercise

Mark off a small area of ground no more than a square metre. Sit and just simply begin to look and notice what you see. Become aware of the variation of colour that is before you, the different tones and intensities and shades. Change your perspective by standing above the spot then moving in much closer by lying on your stomach and looking closely at what you see, again noting the colour variations.

An alternative to this exercise can be looking at a much larger area within your range of vision; for example this could include activities such as watching a sunrise or sunset, or going to a favourite coastal spot and going through the same process of noticing the variation of colour, tones and shades.

With both of these exercises, note your inner responses in terms of your feelings and thoughts, what comes up for you, and write these down, including associations and increased awareness brought about through doing these exercises.

Touch is another important aspect of sensory participation in nature and an embodied form of connection. The focus of exploration is on different feeling senses via the medium of touch. I have often found when I walk barefoot in certain natural locations that my felt sense of connection and embodied contact with nature is heightened, so you may want to do the following exercise barefoot.

Touch exercise

Find a natural location such as woodland, a beach or a favourite spot in nature. Begin to move outwards and seek contact with the natural objects you find, stones, bark, branches, leaves, flowers, etc. Start to get to know them through the use of touch, not only through your hands, but also through other parts of your body such as your face or the soles of your feet. Don't limit yourself to objects but make contact with earth, sand, mud and water through whatever way feels comfortable. Really try to get a sense of the textures and shapes, the sensations invoked through touching nature in all its forms. Note your inner responses in terms of your feelings and thoughts, what comes up for you, and write these down, noting associations and increased awareness brought about through doing these exercises.

Making contact with nature through the medium of taste of course comes with a warning caveat around being careful and knowledgeable about what is dangerous to eat and what is not. I would suggest eating only what you know to be seasonal and if possible locally grown, for example picking edible berries, like blackberries commonly found in the British countryside in late summer.

Taste exercise

Go out and pick some edible berries or fruit such as apples, pears or plums. If you have access to an allotment or garden, pick something grown there which is in season. Note the sense of taste and its intensity, the different aspects of taste and texture of the fruit and vegetables you are eating. Note your inner experiences and write these down.

With the sense of smell, different geographies, seasons and weather conditions will all have an impact and, as with the other participative exercises, it is always good to repeat these through the different seasons.

Smell exercise

Go out into a natural location and begin to focus on your sense of smell. Move between an exploration of passive and active smelling, allowing yourself to be drawn by particular smells and their potential source. Alongside this engage in a more active process of picking up and seeking out particular natural objects, pine cones for example, and of course flowers and blossoms. Note down your inner associations, thoughts and feelings.

With sound, location, geography and weather all come into play. I am particularly drawn to mountainous regions because of the scarcity of man-made sounds which are absent in more remote locations. I find the sound of bird-song, in particular the blackbirds that sing near my house, has the potential to invoke strong feelings within me, depending on what mood I am in. To begin with, I find closing my eyes allows me to tune into sounds a little easier; this is of course dependent of where, when and how you are feeling in the natural setting you have chosen.

Listening exercise

Choose a spot in nature. Begin to tune into the sounds that you are hearing (possibly with eyes closed). Move between an active and passive receiving process. By doing this you can actively focus on specific sounds such as bird-calls, other animal sounds or the sound of the wind moving through the trees, the movement of water, etc. Alternatively you can sit/stand back and just passively receive the sounds, engaging with this as symphony or cacophony perhaps depending on what is going on outside and inside of you. Note down what you feel and what comes up.

Extended wilderness trips and solo time spent in nature

Time spent walking and camping alone in nature can be a very powerful experience on different levels. For some the challenge of camping outdoors, carrying equipment, putting up a tent and sleeping on the ground can provoke strong feelings. For those unused to camping these feelings can include fear and a sense that they are being put through a physical and psychological ordeal. Some of these feelings are dependent on the weather, temperature and the adequacy of the clothing and camping equipment that are being used. If these negative feelings can be sat with, then after a day or two something new begins to emerge, a deeper sense of relaxation, better sleep and more vivid dreams, a greater connection to the natural world and an increased awareness of the feeling process. This has been backed up by research by Hinds (2011) who found that those participating in a wilderness trip in Scotland experienced greater feelings of connection, aliveness, self-discovery and well-being after a ten-day camping and walking trip. The Outward Bound process (Walsh and Gollins 1976) is based on the concept that through facilitated challenges, where specific problem-solving tasks are set, a person can achieve a sense of mastery and self-confidence. The model is akin to adventure therapy ideas and concepts which foreground cognitive and attitudinal processes predominantly with younger client groups. One of the features of the Outward Bound model is the 'solo'; the solo is usually for one or two days, where the participant spends time alone reflecting upon their experience and current direction in life. It is not meant to be an ordeal and can be done with food, or the participant may choose to abstain from food. (The process can be akin to a vision quest but I will say more about this below as this is a specific process aligned more with a deeper spiritual focus.) The 'solo' can be a way of withdrawing from life's distractions in order to facilitate a deeper sense of connection to your inner world through connection to nature. As with any nature-based activity, safety issues need to be considered; these include taking the right equipment, knowing the terrain, knowing how to keep yourself safe and having an exit strategy if anything goes wrong, alongside informing somebody of your plans and location and what to do if you do not return within a specified time.

Using mindfulness in nature

Another way of making contact with yourself through the medium of the natural world is through mindfulness exercises. Mindfulness, as a clinical intervention utilised by therapists in a number of settings, has gained in popularity in recent years. As a regular practice and a way of becoming more present in natural spaces it can be an invaluable tool to develop an understanding of the therapeutic potential of nature for both yourself and your clients.

Mindfulness exercise

Choose a favourite natural spot. Sit and become aware of your breathing and begin to notice your in-breath and your out-breath. Become aware of the contact your body is making with the ground, and your posture by sitting, lying or standing. Notice how your clothes make contact with your skin. Then begin to take your awareness to the sounds around you, in your immediate environment. Then take your awareness further outwards, notice sounds that are far away. Then return to noticing your breathing and if thoughts begin to come into your mind, return to your breathing.

There are variations on this process which focus more specifically on breathing, body awareness and contact, and sounds. You may want to focus more specifically on the process of releasing tension for example.

Focusing in natural environments

Gendlin (1996) is the originator of the focusing approach which consists of six steps to focus the person on an inner awareness of feeling states and how these connect to an outer reality. Gendlin notes these are not a mechanistic 'one-size-fits-all' but act as a vehicle through which the person can focus in on themselves and make links between themselves and their feelings. In the following exercise they are broken down, but as Gendlin says, they need not be separate but may happen concurrently with one another.

Focusing exercise

Find a natural space and then begin to follow these six steps in focusing:

Clearing a space – to relax, begin to focus inwards on your body and begin to focus on the main feeling that arises for you in that moment.

Felt sense – begin to focus in on a problem, but do not get inside it but just begin to notice what it feels like, let it be unclear if need be.

Handle – what does this feel like? Let a word/image come up from the felt sense, stay with the quality of the felt sense until something fits.

Resonate – go back between the felt sense and the word/image checking if there is a bodily signal to let you know where it fits; let the felt sense change: does the word/image fit?

Asking – now ask: what is it, about this whole problem, that makes this quality (which you have just named or pictured)? When it is here again, tap it, touch it, be with it, asking again – what is the felt sense? Be with the felt sense till something comes along with a shift, a slight 'give' or release.

Receiving – receive whatever comes with a shift in a friendly way. Stay with it a while, even if it is only a slight release. Others may come . . . stay with this for a while.

Exploring metaphors of self within nature

A powerful way of exploring aspects of yourself within nature is to explore metaphors you encounter in the natural world and how these resonate with particular aspects of yourself. This can be done in a number of ways, but my favoured process of exploration is to use the four shields devised by Steven Foster and Meredith Little (1998). The four shields correspond to the four compass directions – south, west, north and east; the four seasons – summer, autumn, winter and spring; and the four stages of development – childhood, adolescence, adulthood and elderhood/rebirth.

Four shields exercise

Place four stones or objects on the four compass directions: north, south, east and west. Starting in the south, move around the four directions exploring which resonates with you most strongly (you can choose to walk between directions, e.g. north and south, or around all directions). Walk with a deliberate intent to be open to what you experience. When beginning the walk, mark a gateway or threshold to step through, stating that everything that happens beyond this has meaning for you. When you finish the exercise (one or two hours) step back through a threshold to end the process. Write down what you have experienced, your thoughts, feelings and associations.

Here are the directions:

South – the season is summer, the stage of life is childhood, the psychological processes associated with this direction are embodiment, play, creativity, sexuality.

West – the season is autumn, the stage of life is adolescence, the psychological processes associated with this direction are introspection, self-doubt, our shadow aspects, where conflict may exist.

North – the season is winter, the stage of life is adulthood, the psychological processes associated with this direction are responsibility, providing for ourselves and others, parenthood, finding a career or path in life.

East – the season is spring, the stage of life is elderhood, but also rebirth (because this is a circle), the psychological processes associated with this direction are wisdom, spirituality, transcendence, enlightenment and also healing.

The arts therapies draw upon the idea that symbols, metaphors and processes contained within different arts mediums act as a bridge to the inner world. Sometimes it is difficult to know what we are feeling and by working within a creative medium such as art or music, this allows us to externalise our inner world and in doing so gain access to it at a distance. Using art in a natural context allows this process to become enlivened in relation to living processes that are encountered, through engagement with natural metaphors and materials, which can be used to explore and deepen our understanding of our inner world.

Creativity in nature exercise

Choose a particular theme that you want to explore in your life, for example your relationship with your parents/partner/children, or feelings of loss or sadness, work or career, etc. Choose a natural location, for example woodland, or the sea. Go out with the intent to find or create something to represent this theme in your life. You may choose to stay in one spot and explore your feelings and thoughts through engagement with the materials creating some representation of this. For example you may use stones and driftwood found on the beach and place them by the water's edge, exploring their relationship with the waves and the incoming/outgoing tide. You may bring back a range of natural objects which represent your theme and talk about this with others or write this up in your journal.

Exploring personal/transpersonal processes

Nature provides a space for us to make contact with the deeper mysteries and processes of our life and existence. For some it allows us to make contact with something we experience to be divine or magical. For example, I was recently standing in a glade of trees within a secluded woodland and began to feel a tingling in my body and a strong sense that the trees were alive. I was overcome with a feeling of awe and beauty and a strong sense of interconnection with other living things, the ferns, woodland flowers, fungus and the insects. I experience these feelings more frequently within a natural space, finding it difficult to access this deep connection in my everyday life. Going out and making this sort of connection in natural spaces deepens my sense of connection to a greater sense of spirituality and meaning. For others this need not necessarily be a spiritual or religious thing; it may be much more of an existential connection.

During his personal crisis, Jung would spontaneously draw and create mandalas. He saw the mandala as a representation of the totality of the self, the wholeness of our personality. Jung drew mandalas as a way to gain a living conception of his inner world, his self (Jung 1989: 221). He believed in the power of symbols like mandalas to hold universal meaning (for example the yin and yang symbol). The symbol contains a power to both transform and enliven our understanding of inner psychic process; the mandala can be seen as a symbol which represents the self and can be used as a conduit to gain access to deeper feelings and processes.

Mandala exercise

Choose a natural space and mark out a circle by using natural material such as earth or leaves, etc., or use a stick to draw out a circle. Choose natural objects and materials which you feel drawn to and which may represent and connect with yourself at this time. Notice how you are feeling as you create the mandala; notice the relationships between the different parts, shapes, textures and forms and what they represent in terms of your inner reality and feelings. Reflect upon how your inner reality meets with an outer reality in the creation and symbolism of the natural mandala.

Our ancestors felt an intimate connection to the natural world, which they were dependent on for survival. As practices of hunting and gathering gave way to more organised forms of farming and livestock cultivation, our relationship with nature and our spiritual and religious belief systems shifted to represent these changes. Celebrating the seasons and associated festivals, which occurred at critical points in the year in relation to planting and harvesting, changes in daylight and temperature, allows us to feel a greater sense of connection to the natural world; it also allows us a deeper connection to the personal changes that go on within our own lives as we grow older and change.

Celebrating the seasons

The Celtic wheel of the year contains festivals which correspond with key changes in the seasons.

Yule – midwinter. 21/22 December (in the northern hemisphere) – marks the shortest day and the longest night.
Exercise: Go into nature and find some evergreen plants such as holly, ivy, pine or yew. Light a candle, placing the evergreen leaves or sprigs on a natural altar such as a stone or tree stump. Celebrate the return of the sun as the days begin to lengthen and the nights become shorter; you may choose to light a fire; you may want to mark new beginnings or mark endings of a 'dark' and challenging time. You may want to sit quietly in the dark for some time contemplating this in silence. You may want to think about the relationship between the old and the new, the dark and the light in your life.
Imbolc – early spring. 1/2 February. This is a celebration of the first stirrings of spring, a time of spring cleaning, and may also be a time to make resolutions and dedications for the coming year.
Exercise: Find a natural spot, and seek out any signs of the first blooming of spring and new life, for example the green shoots of crocuses. Take time to sit and connect with the beginnings of new life, both within nature and the beginnings of things within your own life. If you choose to write down or state your intent for the coming year, you may create some ritual to mark this, for example writing this down on a piece of paper and burying it in your garden or in a special place in nature.
Beltane – 1 May. This is a celebration of fertility and growth and marks the beginning of summer. It is traditionally associated with rites such as the maypole dance or the green man.
Exercise: Take some seeds you have previously collected, for example this may be acorns or other seeds you have collected, or alternatively you may want to plant some vegetable or flower seeds in pots. Take time to

prepare the soil either within a seed tray or pot or in the natural spot you have chosen to plant your seeds. Make sure you have chosen some fertile soil or made the soil fertile by using fresh compost. Plant the seeds and sit and reflect upon the creation of new life and growth.

Litha – the summer solstice festival. 20/21 June – when we are at the mid-point of summer and the longest day occurs. This marks the time when the days will begin to grow shorter and the nights longer.

Exercise: Set your alarm clock and wake with the sunrise. Decide a route along which you will walk which will enable you to either return to where you began or be able to use some form of transport to find your way back. Mark your intent, maybe to focus on the balance between light and dark in your life at this time of the year, celebrating the light you have had and preparing for the dark to come. You may want to combine this exercise with the four shields exercise.

Mabon – celebrating the harvest. 21/22 September. During this festival we are celebrating the gathering of the harvest and the time when the stores are full, ready for the coming winter.

Exercise: Go out into nature in search of fruit or berries. If you can find an apple, plum or pear tree, pick the fruit, and give thanks for the bounty of nature and become fully present to the taste, texture and touch of the fruit as you pick and eat it. Reflect upon your inner stores and resources, the emotional and psychological resilience you have gained through experiencing life's challenges.

Samhain – acknowledging the ancestors and marking the beginning of the new year in the pagan calendar. Normally falls around Halloween at the beginning of November. This marks the end of the harvest and beginning of winter. The themes of Samhain are life and death and rebirth.

Exercise: Choose a natural spot and mark out a circle with stones or other natural materials. Sit in the centre of the circle. Focus on what you want to let go of, think of the losses and deaths you have experienced in your life. Think of who and what you want to say goodbye to. This ceremony acknowledges that loss is part of life and in acknowledging and deliberately engaging with what you have lost or want to let go of, can be a very powerful way of inviting something new into your life.

Other festivals:

Ostera/Easter – the spring equinox. Occurs around 17–21 March and will sometimes correspond with Easter. Traditionally a celebration of the lengthening days and within the Christian tradition of rebirth and resurrection.

Lammas/Lughnasadh – traditionally around 1 August, and in Anglo-Saxon times celebrated the bringing in of the wheat harvest, marked by baking bread and giving thanks to the four directions. Contemporary harvest festivals within the Christian tradition happen a little later in the year.

The vision quest

The vision quest is a particular process which can be very intense in terms of the practicalities of participating and setting up a quest, and can appear from the outside as quite extreme, in terms of fasting for three to four days. As a ceremony the vision quest is focused on marking a transition or rite of passage. Because of the nature of the vision quest process and the powerful physical and psychological effects of this process, I would strongly recommend undertaking a quest as part of an organised and facilitated group experience. There are a number of organisations in the USA and Europe which run vision quests and have good reputations for safe, competent and ethical practice. I would recommend the School of Lost Borders in the United States, and there are a number of guides who have trained here who work in Europe. Their website is: www.schooloflostborders.org.

> The vision quest, fasting quest, and all other wilderness rites of passage are but circles drawn in the dust, empty forms to be filled with the unique values and perceptions of the participants, mirrors in which they themselves are reflected.
>
> (Foster and Little 1989: 24)

The history of the vision fast/quest (I will use these terms interchangeably) finds its origins in a variety of sources. The term was taken from Native American tradition, although this type of activity has historically been part of many indigenous cultures around the world. The term has evoked some controversy from Native Americans, so in the United States the term is being used less and less by wilderness trip leaders (Segal 2005).

It is not my intention to give an exhaustive summary of its history, but only to map out the territory and form of the fast. The process of the fast can be seen as a 'container' rooted in mythological, historical and psycho-spiritual contexts. It is a profoundly physical experience which gives rise to both subtle and concrete dimensions of reality, which in turn mirror aspects of the intra- and inter-psychic world of the faster. The experience is then magnified by the inter-relationship with nature.

I will outline the form of the fast, which involves three stages: severance, threshold and incorporation. This form gives birth to the creation of the faster's own 'mono-myth': their own heroic journey. Van Gennep (1960) defined the dynamics of the wilderness fast or rites of passage following a three-phase formula: severance ('separation'), threshold ('marge'), and incorporation ('aggregation'). The modern-day hero quester, creating his/her own mono-myth through the ritual and ceremony of the fast, comes back to a society devoid of meaningful symbols and rituals to celebrate his/her process, to verify his/her new life status and to mark the transition or crisis that he/she has been through. It is precisely this loss of ritual and meaningful ways to mark transitions that the use of rites-of-passage ceremonies is seeking to reverse.

Severance

This is the time for working on one's intent to fast, in preparation for participation in the rite of the vision quest. This clarification of intent to fast is an important part of the process. Davis (2003) proposes that traditionally much of a person's life education provided them with the practical and spiritual tools for a vision quest. For the modern-day quester this process can take up to a year, from first stating their desire to fast to actually partaking in the vision quest.

The mono-mythic journey starts at the end and ends with the beginning, the rebirth. The severance stage is imbued with metaphors and rituals that focus not only on intent to fast, but to mark endings and to think about transitions. What is being left behind? What will one be seeking to mark in this life transition? If the quest is part of overcoming a crisis, what will it take to face the dragon? What rituals will need to be enacted at this stage in order to focus one's intent to understand fully why the fast is being undertaken? All around at this stage are the metaphors of death. What will need to die? What will die within me in order that I can pass through one life stage to the next?

Threshold

> With the personification of his destiny to guide and aid him, the hero goes forward in his adventure until he comes to the 'threshold guardian' at the entrance to the zone of magnified power.
>
> (Campbell 1949: 77)

The threshold guardian for the modern quester normally consists of the person's own fear. Fear of the unknown, the fear of not eating for four days, the fear of being alone in the darkness, fear of the power of nature in the wilderness place. Beyond the fear/threshold guardian lies the unknown: darkness and danger, the myriad projections of the quester's conscious and unconscious fears and terrors. These fears must be faced as the quester moves into the threshold time. This is one of the therapeutic aspects of the fast process, that a fear faced and overcome, terror that can be sat with and looked into, becomes part of the mono-myth. The sense of achievement and bravery involved in participating in this process should not be underestimated. Compared to the months and even years taken in traditional therapy in order to achieve a sense of self-esteem and personal power, the quest can act as a very powerful mobiliser of fear and then a containing space in which the person can find their own sense of themselves. Rituals and exercises performed during the process can act as a way of managing the issues that arise and hold a potentially transformative power for the person engaging and marking a transition in their life.

Threshold begins with a death, a severance (Foster and Little 1992). This part of the creation of the mono-myth in the hero's journey comprises the real ordeal/adventure for the hero. The stage is full of potentially healing emotional states, with the exposure, alone to the elements and to the experience of fasting in a wilderness place.

Incorporation

Incorporation is the phase of return from the experience and understanding the meaning and implications of the ritual you have just undertaken. Steven Foster asks in the *Book of the Vision Quest*: are you prepared to face the consequences you bring back from the sacred mountain? You too will find that if you do not use the treasures you discover you will die a living death. It is dangerous to ask for gramercy from god and do nothing with it; a stark warning about the dangers the quester faces in communing with nature in this way and asking for a vision.

The power of the fast/quest process for the individual lies in its ability to reflect the myths of the world which are then contained in the individual mono-mythic journey, the story of which is given birth to during the fast experience. The gift brought back and shared with the community is a symbol of the transformational power of the fast. All the myths of the world are encompassed in the single journey of the hero quester (Campbell 1949).

Although I would not recommend undertaking a fast without support and a coherent ritual container for the work, which can be provided by an organised group which runs vision quests, you can undertake a mini-version of the quest over a day in a medicine walk exercise.

Medicine walk exercise

This can be undertaken as a mini-version of the vision quest and day solo exercise. Make adequate preparations for a day-long walk in terms of water and other sustenance. There is an option to abstain from food during the walk but obviously this is done at your own discretion and with awareness of the risks and implications. You begin at sunrise and walk in a chosen natural location. Mark a threshold to step across and again when you finish the exercise. You may want to combine this with walking in a particular compass direction or directions depending on where you are and how you will return after your walk. The idea is to wander without any conscious intent on reaching a goal, but to remain alert to what draws your attention and where and what you feel drawn to. Be aware of the symbols and messages that may arise from your contact with mother nature. Keep a journal of the walk. Share this with someone close to you or who can respond in a way that will allow you to explore your story of the walk and dig deeper for its meaning and symbolism.

Concluding comments

In this chapter I have looked at ways in which you can develop your own therapeutic relationship with nature. By exploring your historical relationship with nature and the emotional role it has played in your life you can begin to translate your own experience in order to develop a rationale for taking your therapeutic work outdoors. Several exercises are outlined to develop an engagement with nature through both your senses and your emotional life. Reconnecting to nature overall is an important aspect of feeling how it can affect us on a number of levels and the ways in which it can illuminate our relational struggles and help to heal the splits we may feel between our inner and outer worlds.

References

Campbell, J. (1949) *The Hero with a Thousand Faces*. Princeton, NJ: Princeton University Press.

Davis, J. (1998) The transpersonal dimensions of ecopsychology: nature, non duality and spirit. *The Humanistic Psychologist* 26(1–3), 60–100.

Davis, J. (2003) An overview of transpersonal psychology. *The Humanistic Psychologist* 31(2–3), 6–21.

Foster, S. and Little, M. (1989) *The Roaring of The Sacred River: The Wilderness Quest for Vision and Self Healing*. Big Pine. CA: Lost Borders Press.

Foster, S. and Little, M. (1992) *The Book of The Vision Quest: Personal Transformation in The Wilderness*. New York: Fireside Books.

Foster, S. and Little, M. (1998) *The Four Shields: The Initiatory Seasons of Human Nature*. Big Pine, CA: Lost Borders Press.

Gendlin, E. T. (1996). *Focusing-Oriented Psychotherapy*. New York: Guilford Press.

Hegarty, J. (2010) Out of the consulting room and into the woods? Experiences of nature-connectedness and self-healing. *European Journal of Ecopsychology* 1, 64–84.

Hinds, J. (2011) Exploring the psychological rewards of a wilderness experience: an interpretive phenomenological analysis. *The Humanistic Psychologist* 39, 189–205.

Jung, C. G. (1989) *Memories, Dreams and Reflections*. New York: Knopf.

Mabey, R. (2008) *Nature Cure*. London: Vintage.

Ottosson, J. (2007) The importance of nature in coping: creating increased understanding of the importance of pure experiences of nature to human health. Doctoral thesis, Faculty of Landscape Planning, Horticulture and Agricultural Science, Swedish University of Agricultural Sciences.

Searles, H. (1960) *The Nonhuman Environment: In Normal Development and in Schizophrenia*. New York: International Universities Press.

Segal, F. (2005) Ecopsychology and the uses of wilderness. *Ecopsychology Gatherings*. http://ecp[sychology.athabascau.ca/1097/segal.htm (accessed 17 August 2005).

Shepard, N. (1996) *The Living Mountain: A Celebration of the Cairngorm Mountains of Scotland*. Edinburgh: Canongate Classics.

Tempest-Williams, T. (1991) *Refuge: An Unnatural History of Family and Place*. London: Vintage.

Van Gennep, A. (1960) *The Rites of Passage*. Chicago: University of Chicago Press.

Walsh, V. and Gollins, G. (1976) *An Exploration of the Outward Bound Process.* Denver, CO: Outward Bound Publications.

Wolsko, C. and Hoyt, K. (2012) Employing the restorative capacity of nature: pathways to practicing ecotherapy among mental health professionals. *Ecopsychology* 4(1), 10–24.

Index

Made in the USA
Lexington, KY
09 April 2016